"*Moving from Activity to Achievement* lays out a simple yet powerful process for linking belief and behavior. It's a must read for anyone desiring to improve their performance and productivity; individually or organizationally."

—Dr. Tony Alessandra, Author of *The Platinum Rule*
and Hall-of-Fame Keynote Speaker

******

"This book is packed with principles you can use to take your life and your career to a new level. Chapter 5 alone, on the "Value of Vision," is worth the price of this book."

—Joel Weldon, CPAE, Joel H. Weldon & Associates, Inc.

******

"Only read this book if you are serious about wanting to grow your ability to be more productive and focused. Les Taylor has taken his knowledge and personal experiences, combined it with the knowledge and philosophies of other experts to produce an effective, focused process that will guide you from activity to achievement."

—Steve Padilla, President, Hunter Contracting Company

******

"Les Taylor lays out a simple and easy to apply process for improving performance and productivity. My company used the process with our managers and sales staff in order to make improvements throughout our organization."

—Roger Jeschke, President/CEO, National Pump Company

Moving from Activity to Achievement

Keys for Transforming Your Life and Your Business

LES TAYLOR

iUniverse, Inc.
New York   Bloomington

Moving from Activity to Achievement
Keys for Transforming Your Life and Your Business

Copyright © 2009 Les Taylor

iUniverse books may be ordered through booksellers or by contacting:

iUniverse
1663 Liberty Drive
Bloomington, IN 47403
www.iuniverse.com
1-800-Authors (1-800-288-4677)

ISBN: 978-1-4401-6506-1 (pbk)
ISBN: 978-1-4401-6507-8 (ebk)

Printed in the United States of America

iUniverse rev. date: 9/21/2009

This book is dedicated to my wife Geri and to my family, who have always provided the encouragement and support I needed in my personal and professional efforts toward success and achievement.

The only measure of what you believe is what you do. If you want to know what people believe, don't read what they write, don't ask them what they believe, just observe what they do.

—Ashley Montagu

Contents

Section Three: Purposeful Performance

Section Four: Maintain Alignment

ACKNOWLEDGMENTS

It would be difficult indeed to try and cite all the authorities and sources I used in writing this book. It does, after all, represent more than thirty years of study, personal experience, reading, and talking with many people in many scenarios in this important field of performance improvement. In addition, this book is designed to be a cut-to-the-chase prescription for improving performance and productivity, so citing a page or two of the resources I used to compile this document seems counterproductive.

I do want to acknowledge a few of the people who made the publication of this book possible. Bob Kelly, my editor and owner of WordCrafters, Inc., was both a partner and encourager in bringing this work to fruition. Michelle Ebright, my executive assistant, spent many hours formatting the interior pages. My wife, Geri, provided that second set of eyes I needed to edit the copy.

I sincerely thank each of these dear people for providing the expertise and encouragement I needed to finish this project.

INTRODUCTION

Are you looking for a way to improve performance and productivity, personally or professionally? Do you have that sinking feeling in your heart and mind that whatever you're doing now isn't getting you the results you want in terms of being more focused, more productive, and living a more satisfied life? Then you may just have found what you're looking for.

Moving from Activity to Achievement will introduce you to a very simple but very powerful process for getting you from where you are now to where you want to be. It will change your thinking about success and achievement. It will introduce you to a simple but very powerful methodology for helping you get what you really want out of life.

This book does not contain a silver bullet or magic formula for success and achievement. The reality is that achievement is about doing, not about dreaming. Moving from activity to achievement, from where you are now to where you want to be, will involve many things, not the least of which is a *process*. W. Edwards Deming, one of the great management thinkers of the last century said, "If you can't describe what you're doing as a process, you don't know what you're doing."

The process and principles I developed and describe in this book are a compilation of many things I've learned over the years. Some I learned through formal education, some I learned through personal experience, and some I learned by specifically studying performance improvement for more than thirty years.

Moving from Activity to Achievement is a simple but powerful method for helping you or your organization get from where you are now to where you want to be. Even more powerful, however, than the six steps and three principles described in this book is the philosophy upon which the process is based. That philosophy says that belief manifests itself in behavior.

What you and I believe, I mean really believe deep down inside the recesses of our heart and mind, will be shown in what we do. By any measure, what we say we believe about virtually anything will be shown to the world in what we actually do on a consistent basis.

Our commitment to our health and well-being will be demonstrated by our eating and exercise habits. Our commitment to our marriage and our family will be demonstrated in how much time we spend with them and how we treat them when we're home. Our commitment to our own personal growth and development will be demonstrated in the things we do, the materials we read, the degree to which we educate ourselves in the practice, and the principles of self or organizational development.

Moving from Activity to Achievement, therefore, is about process and about philosophy. We must have some vehicle, some methodology, for taking us from where we are now to a better place, in terms of improved performance and productivity. That's what this book will do for you. It will reinforce what you already know about the value of linking belief and behavior. *Moving from Activity to Achievement* will change your thinking about why you do what you do. At the same time, it will inspire you to apply the process and principles in this book to every aspect of your life, personally and professionally.

Section One: Activity to Achievement

CHAPTER 1

Why Aren't We More Productive?

It is never too late to be
what you might have been.
~ George Eliot

Have you ever asked yourself why you aren't as successful as you want to be? Or, why your business or organization isn't more successful than it is? Have you ever wondered "Why is so-and-so able to accomplish so much in such a short period of time and I'm not?" Sure you have, and guess what? We all have.

I'm convinced that if we conducted a national survey, we'd find that most people, and most organizations, feel they aren't performing at the level they could or should. They look at other individuals or other organizations, compare them to themselves and what they've accomplished, and get depressed very quickly at the disparity between where they are and where they want to be.

At speaking engagements or media interviews, I'm often asked why people don't accomplish more than they do, or why so many businesses and organizations fail. While there's no short answer to this type of question, there are some realities I can share, both from personal experience and from studying personal achievement and performance improvement for more than thirty years, which can shed some light on this all too common problem.

Here are five reasons why we're not achieving greater levels of success and achievement:

Reason #1 - Lack of Desire

Desire is something more than wanting or wishing or hoping we'll be more successful, or that our business or organization will produce whatever product or service it was built to produce.

The reality is that no one ever wished his or her way to success and achievement. Success is about doing, not dreaming. Desire is that fire in the belly that causes us to do those things that need to be done to reach a specific level of success or achieve a particular objective.

> *"The starting point of all achievement is desire. Keep this constantly in mind. Weak desire brings weak results, just as a small amount of fire makes a small amount of heat."*
> ~ Napoleon Hill

Every story you'll ever read about some outstanding accomplishment reached or an incredible goal achieved also speaks to desire. That inner push or pull, that book that must be written, or the job that must be had, that goal that must be reached despite all the odds against its probability of happening, is desire.

Napoleon Hill, in his landmark book *Think and Grow Rich*, said, "Every person who wins in any undertaking must be willing to burn his ships and cut all sources of retreat. Only by doing so can one be sure of maintaining that state of mind known as a burning desire to win, essential to success."

On a scale of one to ten, rate your level of desire to be more successful, increase your productivity, or improve your performance. Remember, desire is more than just wishing or hoping something better will happen. Desire causes us to say, "I'm going to do what I have to do, to accomplish what I want to accomplish. I'll pay the price I have to pay to get from where I am now to where I want to be."

Rate Your Level of Desire
1 2 3 4 5 6 7 8 9 10

Reason #2 - Failing to Take Personal Initiative

Here's a cold, hard fact; no one else is going to take responsibility for your personal growth, or your personal success, or for seeing to it that you accomplish whatever you say you want to accomplish, and no one else should. That responsibility belongs to you, and you alone.

Failing to take personal responsibility for the results we want, personally or professionally, may be the single greatest reason for failure, for lack of promotion, poor performance, low self-esteem, and for failed relationships.

> *"When an archer misses the mark, he turns and looks for the fault within himself. Failure to hit the bull's eye is never the fault of the target. To improve your aim— improve yourself."*
> ~ Gilbert Arland

Unfortunately, the blame game is a popular sport these days. It's popular because it's easy to play! It's so much easier to blame someone else or something else for our poor performance. It's that lousy boss I have; it's the poor economy; it's too cold; it's too hot; the commissions are too low; the market's too crowded; I didn't get the training I needed.

If lack of desire is the primary cause for minimal success and achievement, not taking personal responsibility for why things are the way they are is a very close second. We live in a time when playing the role of a victim is not only acceptable but encouraged. Pointing to anyone or anything else as the reason behind our current state of affairs will hamstring our ability to move forward.

Are you playing the blame game? Or are you putting forth the initiative required to take your performance and productivity to the next level?

Rate Your Level of Personal Initiative
1 2 3 4 5 6 7 8 9 10

Reason #3 - Lack of a Performance Improvement Process

Why is having a process for improving performance and productivity so important? Because process adds form and function to our desires and our ideas.

> *"If you can't describe what you're doing as a process, you don't know what you're doing."*
> — *W. Edwards Deming, one of the great management thinkers of the last century.*

Without a process for improving performance and productivity, we're leaving the possibility for success and achievement to chance. We're hoping something good will happen, or we'll find the silver bullet that will transform our current condition or status into something better.

That isn't going to happen. Personal improvement is the result of doing certain things a certain way, every day. Luck isn't part of the equation. Being diligent at following a process is.

When I decided to write this book, I knew I needed a process for making it happen. I did some research, chose the methodology that made the most sense to me, and started using the process, step by step.

You purchased this book because you wanted to change the status quo. My guess is that you realize whatever method or methods you're currently using for improving performance and productivity simply aren't working.

> *Personal improvement is the result of doing certain things a certain way, every day.*

My second guess is that you don't have a process for getting you from where you are now to where you want to be. Without a map and a compass, you'll have little chance of reaching the land of performance improvement.

Rate Your Process for Improvement
1 2 3 4 5 6 7 8 9 10

Reason #4 - Lack of Commitment

Commitment to what? I mean commitment to personal improvement and commitment to a process in order to make sure you achieve what you want to achieve.

Jim Rohn, billed as America's foremost business philosopher, talks about the reasons for failure and for success. Jim says failure is the result of a few errors in judgment repeated every day, and success is the result of a few simple disciplines practiced every day.

"There's a difference between interest and commitment. When you're interested in doing something, you do it only when circumstances permit. When you're committed to something, you accept no excuses, only results."
—Art Turock

Just trying something for a day or two, or for a week, won't create the habits for success and achievement you'll need to create. Commitment to getting better is essential, because some days are better than others, some things don't work the way we want them to, and people will sometimes let us down.

We have to commit to doing certain things in a certain way every day. We also have to commit to some type of a process for improvement, and then trust that process if we want to get better doing whatever we're doing. Your personal commitment to self-improvement, and to a process for improvement, are critical to your success.

We have to commit to some type of a process for improvement, and then trust that process if we want to get better doing whatever we're doing.

Rate Your Level of Commitment
1 2 3 4 5 6 7 8 9 10

Reason #5 - Lack of Accountability

Accountability is the missing link in putting together a performance improvement program, but a link that is truly essential for ensuring we stay focused on those things that matter most.

> *"Accountability breeds response-ability."*
> —Stephen R. Covey

This is the heart of every personal or professional coaching plan in existence today. Why? Because we all need a little help staying focused and motivated. You'll hear me say more than once that performance improvement is a team sport. While you have to take the responsibility for your success and achievement, you'll also need some help along the way. It's just too easy to get caught up in the grind, or to start majoring on those minor things that rob us of real achievement. We've all experienced the benefit of having someone to support and encourage our most important activities. Admit or not, we need someone on the sidelines shouting or whispering words of encouragement.

Accountability starts by holding our own feet to the fire to do the things we need to do in order to accomplish what we want to accomplish.

Accountability starts by holding our own feet to the fire to do the things we need to do in order to accomplish what we want to accomplish. But it's also important to have a spouse, friend, or colleague hold us accountable as well.

Sharing our desire with someone we trust, and sharing with that person the process we intend to follow to achieve our goals, will go a long way in helping us to achieve the success we want to have.

Accountability works in a team environment as well.

Rate Your Level of Accountability
1 2 3 4 5 6 7 8 9 10

It's All About You

So, how did you relate to the five reasons for not performing at a higher level?

1. Does your level of desire need a boost?

2. Are you ready to take personal responsibility for your growth and development?

3. Do you have a process for improving your performance and productivity?

4. Are you ready to commit to self-improvement?

5. Are you ready to ask a friend to hold you accountable for developing a few new success habits?

In the next chapter, I'll introduce you to a simple but powerful process for taking your current level of performance and productivity to a whole new level.

More Thoughts on Improving Performance

"Initiative is to success what a lighted match is to a candle."
—Orlando A. Battista

"Hold yourself responsible for a higher standard than anybody expects of you. Never excuse yourself."
—Henry Ward Beecher

"People who are unable to motivate themselves must be content with mediocrity, no matter how impressive their other talents."
—Andrew Carnegie

"Take the initiative, take it yourself, take the step with your will now, make it impossible to go back. Burn your bridges behind you. … Make the thing inevitable."
—Oswald Chambers

"You need to feel good about yourself, the motivation has to come from within. You have nobody to fall back on except yourself."

—Dana Hill

"The key that unlocks energy is desire. It's also the key to a long and interesting life. If we expect to create any drive, any real force within ourselves, we have to get excited."

—Earl Nightingale

"Our plans miscarry because they have no aim. When you don't know what harbor you're aiming for, no wind is the right wind."

—Seneca

CHAPTER 2

There Is a Solution

*The principles you live by
create the world you live in;
if you change the principles you live by,
you will change your world.*
~ Blaine Lee

In the last chapter, we discussed the five reasons more people and organizations aren't more successful than they are. They lack desire, fail to take personal responsibility and initiative, don't have a process for improving performance and productivity, aren't committed to their own success or a process for achieving success and, lastly, don't have an accountability mechanism to help them stay focused and on track.

In this chapter, I want to introduce you to a time-tested process for moving you from activity to achievement. While the process itself is incredibly powerful, the principles behind the process are equally powerful as well.

The Principles

By definition, a principle is a basic truth or law or assumption. The principle of gravity, for example, says that, when dropped, an object will always go down, it will never go in the opposite direction.

A principle can also be thought of as a basic generalization that is accepted as true and can be used as a basis for reasoning or conduct.

The Principle of Perspective

The first principle in the model for performance improvement is the principle of perspective. Perspective means observing something from a particular vantage point or in its relationship to something else.

The higher we climb in a plane, for example, the more of the horizon we see. While we're sitting on the tarmac, our view of the horizon is severely limited but, at fifty thousand feet, we can actually see the curvature of the earth.

In terms of performance improvement, the principle of perspective has to do with our belief system, personally or professionally. Since most agree that belief will manifest itself in behavior, it's important for us to be very clear on what we believe, so we can judge our behavior accordingly.

We clarify our perspective by clarifying our vision, our mission, and our values. Vision describes what we want to become, what we want to accomplish, or what results we expect to produce. If our vision is clear of what we want to accomplish, we have a much greater chance of succeeding in bringing that vision to fruition.

> *We clarify our perspective by clarifying our vision, our mission, and our values.*

The Principle of Performance

The second powerful principle for moving from activity to achievement is the principle of performance.

In this instance, performance doesn't have anything to do with acting. It has everything to do with achievement, accomplishment, and results. It's about execution. It's about carrying a plan to action.

Strategies, Goals and Actions

> *Performance doesn't have anything to do with acting. It has everything to do with achievement, accomplishment, and results.*

The three elements of the principle of performance in moving from activity to achievement are strategies, goals, and actions.

Strategies are grand ideas and big picture plans for what we want to achieve in a specific field or category. We'll talk about developing sales strategies for our business, for example, or for developing specific personal or professional development strategies. Strategies provide direction for the goals that we'll set and for the actions we'll take.

Goals are those measurable objectives that power our plan of action. Goals are dreams with a deadline. Every goal must be measurable. Our goals will provide the yardsticks by which we measure our progress.

Actions are those specific tasks we must accomplish in order to achieve our goals. Actions, like goals, must be measurable but, unlike goals, are proximate, short term and quickly accomplished.

The Principle of Alignment

The third and last principle we use in our quest to move from activity to achievement is the principle of alignment.

Using this principle, we'll set in motion processes for making sure our belief (perspective) and our behavior (performance) are in sync.

Alignment has to do with adjustment and readjustment. The reason for the need for alignment? Because things change, and in our world things change pretty quickly and pretty often.

I'm not talking about our values changing or our mission changing, but our circumstances change frequently. Markets change, the economy changes, our customers move or go out of business and, of course, our personal and professional circumstances change.

Alignment is about making those necessary course adjustments to accommodate, adjust, or readjust for the curve balls that life throws at us from time to time. As Spencer Johnson reminds us in his national best selling book, *Who Moved My Cheese?*, change happens, so anticipate change, monitor change, change, enjoy change, and be ready to quickly change again and again.

That's why we need to maintain alignment during the process of moving from activity to achievement.

Alignment is about making those necessary course adjustments to accommodate, adjust, or readjust for the curve balls that life throws at us from time to time.

Are You Ready?

If you're tired of plodding along and not getting the results you know you're capable of getting, then you have the right book in your hand.

I look forward to helping you move your life or your business from activity to achievement as you discover the keys for transforming your life or your business.

More Thoughts on Productivity

"Whatever your present environment may be, you will fall, remain or rise with your thoughts, your vision, your ideal. You will become as small as your controlling desire; as great as your dominant aspiration."

—James Lane Allen

"As soon as you've made a reasonable decision, based on factual information, the time has come for action."

—Nolan Bushnell

"Since changes are going on anyway, the great thing is to learn enough about them so that we will be able to lay hold of them and turn them in the direction of our desires."

—John Dewey

"Without goals, and plans to reach them, you are like a ship that has set sail with no destination."

—Fitzhugh Dodson

"The world recognizes nothing short of performance, because performance is what it needs and promises are of no use to it."

—Phillip G. Hamerton

"The vision must be followed by the venture. It is not enough to stare up the steps—we must step up the stairs."

—Vance Havner

"If you are wedded to today's trends, you'll be widowed by the weekend."

—E. Stanley Jones

"Aim for a star, and keep your sights high! With a heart full of faith within, your feet on the ground, and your eyes in the sky."

—Helen Lowrie Marshall

"The tragedy in life doesn't lie in not reaching your goal. The tragedy lies in having no goal to reach."

—Dr. Benjamin E. Mays

"Change is always powerful. Let your hook be always cast. In the pool where you least expect it, will be a fish."

—Ovid

CHAPTER 3

The Power of a Plan

Make no little plans;
they have no magic to stir the blood.
Make big plans, aim high in hope and work.
~ Daniel Burnham

Jim Horan, author and developer of *The One Page Business Plan*, says the most important reason to have a plan is to clarify thinking. I couldn't agree more.

The power of having a performance improvement plan, or some type of business plan, is to clarify your thinking and to focus your activity.

Engineers discovered millenniums ago that if they were able to harness a meandering river, for example, and channel its flow, they could make the river work for them, instead of the other way around.

Three thousand years ago, Solomon, a pretty successful king in ancient Israel, said, "There's nothing new under the sun." Solomon was referring to the fallacy of chasing after things that really don't bring true happiness. Or worse yet, just chasing!

> *Developing a plan, like the one I'm recommending in this book, is like handing you a road map for success and achievement.*

That concept was true then and it's true now, especially regarding the issue of being very clear on what matters most, and what you really want to achieve, personally or professionally. Developing a plan, like the one I'm recommending in this book, is like handing you a road map for success and achievement.

I'm a subscriber and a big fan of *Success* magazine. In virtually every issue, every success story, and in almost every article on success and achievement, this idea of developing clarity about what you want to accomplish and having a plan to do so is reinforced.

Focus and clarity are synonymous. I read somewhere once that FOCUS stands for Follow One Course Until Successful. Nothing is more damaging to your ability to get things done than letting distractions knock you off course.

A low level of focus will result in substandard performance and a low level of productivity. Conversely, a high level of focus will result in a high level of action and a high level of productivity

Here are areas where you want to make sure you have clarity and focus:

> *Nothing is more damaging to your ability to get things done than letting distractions knock you off course.*

- **Your Vision.** What do you want to accomplish? What long-term goal do you want to achieve? Can you see it clearly in your mind's eye? Can you describe it in very succinct terms?

- **Your Mission.** Your mission describes why you're doing what you're doing. Mission describes the fundamental reason for your existence, personally or organizationally.

- **Your Values.** Values don't mean much unless they're linked to specific behaviors. Why? Because what we say we value must be seen in our behavior to be believed.

- **Strategy (Plans).** That view from ten thousand feet where you see what you want to accomplish and have described the methods by which you'll bring your vision to fruition.

- **Goals.** Describe how you'll measure your progress in accomplishing the plans you've made for success and achievement.

- **Actions.** You have a plan and you've set important objectives (goals), now what must you actually do to have a successfully completed plan?

No Plan, No Power

There's no magic formula to success and achievement, but there's a long-standing technique for rising above the crowd when it comes to improved performance and productivity. Be clear on those things that matter most, then carve out time to attend to them. It's that simple and that profound.

You'll be hard pressed to find any successful individual or any vibrant organization that doesn't have a plan. Your success and achievement won't come about by accident, but will be the result of harnessing your meandering energies and efforts. Your plan for moving from activity to achievement provides the channel and the clarity you'll need for succeeding at just about anything you choose to do.

1. Do you have a plan in place to match your vision for success and achievement?

2. Are you committed to following that plan in spite of the circumstances?

3. Are you willing to do the work necessary to bring your plan and ultimately your vision to fruition?

More Thoughts on Planning

"We can't cross a bridge until we come to it; but I always like to lay down a pontoon ahead of time."
—Bernard M. Baruch

"The method of the enterprising is to plan with audacity, and execute with vigor, to sketch out a map of possibilities, and then to treat them as probabilities."
—Christian N. Bovée

"The future that we study and plan for begins today."
—Chester O. Fischer

"First comes thought; then organization of that thought, into ideas and plans; then transformation of those plans into reality. The beginning, as you will observe, is in your imagination."
—Napoleon Hill

"He who every morning plans the transactions of the day and follows out that plan carries a thread that will guide him through the labyrinth of the most busy life."
—Victor Hugo

"A goal without a plan is just a wish."

—Antoine de Saint-Exupéry

"The important thing is to start, to lay a plan and then follow it step-by-step no matter how small or large each step by itself may seem."

—Robert Louis Stevenson

"Apathy can be overcome by enthusiasm, and enthusiasm can be aroused by two things: first, an idea which takes the imagination by storm; and second, a definite, intelligible plan for carrying that idea into action."

—Arnold J. Toynbee

"An intelligent plan is the first step to success. The man who plans knows where he is going, knows what progress he is making and has a pretty good idea of when he will arrive. Planning is the open road to your destination. If you don't know where you are going, how can you expect to get there?"

—Basil S. Walsh

CHAPTER 4

Activity vs. Achievement

*Some can't distinguish between
being busy and being productive.
They are human windmills,
flailing at work, but actually
accomplishing little.*
~ Caroline Donnelly

We'll start our move from activity to achievement by, as usual, going over the basics. Vince Lombardi, the legendary coach of the Green Bay Packers, used to start each summer's preseason training sessions by focusing on the basics. On the first day of training, Coach Lombardi would gather the team together, hold the pigskin up in the air, and say, "Gentlemen, this is a football."

Why make such a statement to a group of players who were recognized world champions? Because Vince Lombardi understood that fundamentals are the cornerstone of success. Just running around the field tackling people isn't going to result in any kind of success.

One of the fundamental realities of performance improvement is that activity and achievement are not the same thing.

One of the fundamental realities of performance improvement is that activity and achievement are not the same thing. It would be a huge mistake to assume there's a direct correlation between activity and accomplishment, between activity and productivity, or between activity and achievement.

There are, in fact, clear contrasts between the two:

Activity	Achievement
Energetic Movement	Planned Movement
Situational	Principle Based
Short Term	Long Term/Enduring
Random Acts of Progress	Strategic, Sustained Progress

Activity produces *energetic movement*. I'll bet it's not too difficult to picture yourself bouncing from one activity to another, like the silver ball in a pinball machine. You're going nine-hundred miles an hour with your hair on fire, but you're not productive, you're just *busy*.

The fact is that most of our day is committed to activity. We hit the ground running and we don't stop for the next eight to twelve hours. But being busy and being productive are, more often than not, mutually exclusive.

Achievement, on the other hand, results from *planned movement*. It involves being busy, doing the things that matter most. Planned activity results in productivity. It's not the number of things we get done in a day that counts, it's about staying focused on what's really important.

It's not the number of things we get done in a day that counts, it's about staying focused on what's really important.

Activity is *situational*; it's subject to the pressing and the proximate. One of the common terms for this malady is "putting out fires." It results from getting caught up in the crisis of the day. It's the ringing phone, the knock on the door, and the fateful question, "Do you have a minute?"

The definition of crisis is: a dangerous situation developed suddenly. The danger of constantly responding to the crisis du jour is the time lost by not being able to focus on the work of bringing a vision or a goal to fruition.

Achievement doesn't result from being crisis driven. Achievement results from being principle focused. In a sense, it's being idealistic. It means living, acting, and reacting for the greater good. It means looking beyond all those little things, and focusing on the things that are important, but not urgent.

Activity is *short term*. Most of the activity of the day results in very little sustained productivity. Oh, we might make a little progress but, when all the feathers hit the floor, the progress will be short term and our level of performance will be limited indeed.

When our focus, however, is on achievement, we can plan for those daily interruptions. We expect the crisis to come, but we're not thrown off course because of it. As a result, our production and performance take on a long-term perspective.

Activity produces what I refer to as random acts of progress. We may make a few strides and enjoy a limited amount of success, but it won't be strategic or sustained. Based on the issues we've already discussed in this section alone, you can see why activity can only produce random progress.

Achievement produces *strategic and sustained progress.* Because our activity and our energy are predicated on a process and are principle driven, our progress becomes strategic and sustained.

Bear in mind that one of the basics of improved performance and productivity is understanding that activity and achievement are two different things and will ultimately produce different results. Activity produces frustration and failure. Achievement produces joy and fulfillment.

So Which Will It Be, Activity or Achievement?

1. Are you one of those folks going hard from dawn to dusk but not getting much accomplished?

2. Are most of the decisions you make each day based on circumstance or principle?

3. Are the effects of your daily decisions short-term, or are they designed to move beyond the current crisis?

4. Are you making random acts of progress, or will your progress be sustained and enduring because of a long-range view?

Keep reading! All you need is a plan for refocusing your life and your priorities.

More Thoughts on Activity vs. Achievement

"A molehill man is a pseudo-busy executive who comes to work at 9 AM and finds a molehill on his desk. He has until 5 PM to make this molehill into a mountain. An accomplished molehill man will have his mountain finished before lunch."

—Fred Allen

"The weakest living creature, by concentrating his powers on a single object, can accomplish something; whereas the strongest, by dispersing his over many, may fail to accomplish anything."

—Thomas Carlyle

"It is so easy to confuse our daily busyness with our daily business. Many of us earn our living in business, but waste much of the rest of our time on busyness that profits us little."

—David Dunn

"If we would only give, just once, the same amount of reflection to what we want to get out of life that we give to the question of what to do with a two weeks' vacation, we would be startled at our false standards and the aimless procession of our busy days."

—Dorothy Canfield Fisher

"It is more important to know where you are going than to get there quickly. Do not mistake activity for achievement."

—Mabel Newcomber

"Beware the barrenness of a busy life!"

—Socrates

"Have you noticed that even the busiest people are never too busy to take time to tell you how busy they are?"

—Bob Talbert

"It is not enough to be busy; so are the ants. The question is: What are we busy about?"

—Henry David Thoreau

"How you are busy is not as important as why you are busy. The bee is praised. The mosquito is swatted."

—Anonymous

Section Two: Developing Perspective

CHAPTER 5

The Value of Vision

*A rock pile ceases to be a rock pile
the moment a single man contemplates it,
bearing within him the image of a cathedral.*
~ Antoine de Saint-Exupéry

Vision means seeing what could be, as opposed to what is. It's that clear mental picture of a desired outcome. The value of vision is found not in the vision itself, but in what we do with what we see in our mind's eye. Seeing the cathedral is of little value if we don't take the actions necessary to transform the rock pile.

Vision describes *what you're going to do* to improve performance and productivity. Vision also clarifies the *changes* that must take place to get you from where you are now to where you want to be.

Vision differs from strategy. The former sees the preferred future. The latter is an actual plan for bringing the vision to fruition.

Seeing What Could Be

What's your vision for improved performance and productivity? What are some of the things you could actually do to start your move from activity to achievement, or start improving your company's performance and productivity?

Here are some questions that may jump-start the thinking process:

Personally

What are three things I'm doing now that are actually hindering me from accomplishing my vision?

1.

2.

3.

What should I stop doing, or at least do less of, that's hindering my success and achievement?

1.

2.

3.

What are three things I should *start* doing that will improve my current situation?

1.

2.

3.

Professionally/Corporately

What product or service could I/we provide that is not being provided now?

What changes will need to take place to make our business more effective or productive?

What three things do we need to *start* doing, or do *more of*, that will significantly improve our product line or service delivery?

1.

2.

3.

What industry do we intend to serve?

What's our target market?

Fill in the Gaps: See Where You Want to Be

Developing an inspiring and motivating vision statement is the first step in clarifying your perspective. It's like pulling out a map,

When you get specific about what you want to accomplish, the chances of successfully completing the journey more than double.

spreading it out on a table, identifying where you are now, placing your finger on the spot where you want to be, and seeing clearly how to get there.

You see the distances that must be taken into account; you see the hills, the mountains, and the valleys that must be crossed to reach your intended destination. The key, however, is that you're now able to visualize the trip.

When you get specific about what you want to accomplish, the chances of successfully completing the journey more than double.

Note the difference between the following two statements:

"Someday I hope to start my own consulting practice."

"By December 31, 2010, I will have grown Mark Freeman and Associates into a $250,000 a year, Dallas-based consulting practice, specializing in change management for small to medium-sized companies in the medical services industry."

I think you can easily see not only the difference between the two, but the power the second statement has because of its clarity and focus.

We won't wish our way to success and achievement any more than a ship will drift into an intended port of call.

Timelines are formulated, dollar amounts are specified, and the nature of the business, as well as the target market, is clear. The vision statement is short but concise. It's easy for the owner of the vision to see the course ahead. It's easy to share a vision such as this with others who will have a part in bringing the vision to reality.

Too Important to Be Left to Chance

Our futures are too important to be left to chance. We won't wish our way to success and achievement any more than a ship will drift into an intended port of call.

Of all the creatures on the planet, we alone are able to create a vision for what could be, and then use our intelligence, skills, abilities, and talents to create a new reality for ourselves and others.

Now It's Your Turn

1. Take the time necessary to sit down and write a personal or organizational vision statement that will clearly define what you intend to accomplish.

2. Share your vision with a trusted colleague or friend.

3. Remember, your vision could change. You may have to make necessary adjustments, but write your statement and start building that cathedral which, until today, has been nothing but a pile of rocks.

More on the Value of Vision

"The vision that you glorify in your mind, the ideal that you enthrone in your heart—this you will build your life by, this you will become."

—James Lane Allen

"Be daring, be different, be impractical; be anything that will assert integrity of purpose and imaginative vision against the play-it-safers, the creatures of the commonplace, the slaves of the ordinary."

—Cecil Beaton

"A blind man's world is bounded by the limits of his touch; an ignorant man's world by the limits of his knowledge; a great man's world by the limits of his vision."

—E. Paul Hovey

"The idea is to seek a vision that gives you purpose in life and then to implement that vision."

—Lewis P. Johnson

"There are so many wonderful things in your everyday experience, lucrative opportunities, glorious occasions, that do not exist for you because you do not have the vision for discerning them."

—Edward Kramer

"Two men look out through the same bars: One sees the mud, and one the stars."

—Frederick Langbridge

"A vision foretells what may be ours. It is an invitation to do something. With a great mental picture in mind we go from one accomplishment to another, using the materials about us only as steppingstones to that which is higher and better and more satisfying."

—Katherine Logan

"Vision is the world's most desperate need. There are no hopeless situations, only people who think hopelessly."

—Winifred Newman

CHAPTER 6

❀

The Magic of Mission

When you discover your mission,
you will feel its demand.
It will fill you with enthusiasm and
a burning desire to get to work on it.
—W. Clement Stone

Mission defines the fundamental purpose for your existence. It describes why you do what you do. Your mission tells you, and everyone else associated with you, why you get up in the morning and why you go to work.

Mission defines the fundamental purpose for your existence. It describes why you do what you do. Your mission tells you, and everyone else associated with you, why you get up in the morning and why you go to work.

I use the words mission and purpose synonymously. Typically, I associate mission with a business function and purpose with an individual. Both, however, answer the "why" question. The magic of mission is that it describes the philosophy behind your actions and activities.

If you manage or own a business, your mission is not, in my view, a description of your product or service. Your mission is not a description of what you intend to achieve or become. You described that in your vision. Your mission is your compass, personally and organizationally.

Missions with Meaning

As a business consultant and executive coach, I've seen it all when it comes to vision and mission statements. I've seen vision statements that are really mission statements and vice versa. There seems to be a lot of confusion as to the difference between the two.

Here are a couple of examples of mission statements that do a great job of describing the underlying purpose of the organization:

The Disney Corporation: Make People Happy. Actually, the entire statement is, "Using our imaginations to make people happy."

Notice the mission doesn't say anything about theme parks, cartoons, cartoon characters, movies, or any of that. It simply describes the final outcome of their efforts—*happiness.*

How about the Ritz-Carlton hotel chain? Do you know what their mission is? "Ladies and Gentlemen—Serving Ladies and Gentlemen."

I especially like this one because it sends such a powerful message to employees and to customers. That statement not only describes their overarching purpose for existence, it also describes the culture they want to create in the organization and the target market they want to serve.

See what I mean? Your mission statement should tell you and everyone else inside and outside your business why you exist.

The Power of Personal Purpose

Rick Warren, the founding pastor of Saddleback Church in Lake Forest, California, and the best-selling author of *The Purpose Driven Life*, identifies five benefits of leading a purpose driven life:

> *Mission gives meaning to our lives and our businesses. Without a clear mission, you and I would not develop the commitment we need to accomplish what we say we want to accomplish.*

1. Knowing your purpose gives meaning to your life.

2. Knowing your purpose simplifies your life.

3. Knowing your purpose focuses your life.

4. Knowing your purpose motivates your life.

5. Knowing your purpose prepares you for eternity.

Instead of just following the crowd and doing what everyone else is doing, you become focused and on course. You're no longer drifting with the wind. While everyone else is bouncing from one activity to another, you're able to channel time and activity into doing those things that will bring your vision to fruition.

Mission gives meaning to our lives and our businesses. Without a clear mission, you and I would not develop the commitment we need to accomplish what we say we want to accomplish.

The power of mission lies in the commitment we have to that mission. It's all too easy to craft some idealistic reason for doing what we do. It's quite another matter, however, to use our mission or purpose to inspire outstanding service.

Now It's Your Turn

1. Craft a purpose statement or organizational mission statement that paints a picture of why you do what you do.

2. In crafting an organizational mission statement, try not to describe a product or service. Instead, like Disney or Ritz-Carlton, explain why you do what you do.

3. Mull your statement over for a while. Make sure it's genuine. Don't draft a statement you think others will admire. Write a statement that truly explains why you do what you do.

More Thoughts on Perspective

"Above all, be of single aim; have a legitimate and useful purpose, and devote yourself unreservedly to it."
—James Lane Allen

"The secret of success is constancy to purpose."
—Benjamin Disraeli

"That business mission is so rarely given adequate thought is perhaps the most important single cause of business frustration."
—Peter F. Drucker

"A strong will, a settled purpose, an invincible determination, can accomplish almost anything; and in this lies the distinction between great men and little men."
—Thomas Fuller

"Great minds have purposes, others have wishes. Little minds are tamed and subdued by misfortune; but great minds rise above them."
—Washington Irving

"If you want to take your mission in life to the next level, if you're stuck and you don't know how to rise, don't look outside yourself. Look inside. Don't let your fears keep you mired in the crowd. Abolish your fears and raise your commitment level to the point of no return, and I guarantee you that the Champion within will burst forth to propel you toward victory."

—Bruce Jenner

"You can have anything you want—if you want it badly enough. You can be anything you want to be, do anything you set out to accomplish if you hold to that desire with singleness of purpose."

—Abraham Lincoln

"I am here for a purpose and that purpose is to grow into a mountain, not to shrink to a grain of sand."

—Og Mandino

"A purpose is the eternal condition of success."

—Theodore T. Munger

"A determinate purpose in life and a steady adhesion to it through all disadvantages, are indispensable conditions of success."

—William M. Punshion

"Singleness of purpose is one of the chief essentials for success in life, no matter what may be one's aim."

—John D. Rockefeller

"Nothing contributes so much to tranquilizing the mind as a steady purpose—a point on which the soul may fix its intellectual eye."

—Mary Wollstonecraft Shelley

"Every life should have a purpose to which it can give the energies of its mind and the enthusiasms of its heart. That life without a purpose will be prey to the perverted ways waiting for the uncommitted life."

—C. Neil Strait

CHAPTER 7

The Value of Values

It's not hard to make decisions
when you know what your values are.
~ Roy Disney

Values are the third element of developing perspective. Jim Collins and Jerry I. Porras, in their best-selling business book, *Built to Last*, define values as "those guiding principles that help organizations navigate the murky waters of the corporate world."

In their search to discover why some corporations were able to stand the tests of time when so many others were not, they discovered the commitment that enduring companies had to a set of core values. These non-negotiable enduring principles defined the very character of the organization.

In addition to defining character, values define acceptable behavior, individually and organizationally. In reality, a value isn't a value unless it's seen in behavior.

Values describe our internal belief system. Values are intrinsic. They require no external justification. They're right because they're right and need no further justification.

> *In addition to defining character, values define acceptable behavior, individually and organizationally.*

The value of a value lies in the behavior it generates. A value in the sense we're describing in this chapter isn't just a word. It describes how we intend to act or behave, personally or organizationally.

There's a great story of a Ritz-Carlton employee who was asked for a glass of water by a delivery person on the loading dock of the hotel. The employee disappeared for a few minutes and returned with a crystal glass, filled with sparkling water, ice, and a slice of lemon. She served the water to the deliveryman, along with a linen napkin which she placed in his hand, as if he were seated in the hotel's main dining room.

When asked why she went to such trouble to provide the glass of water, she replied that it was no trouble whatsoever and that any Ritz employee would have provided this same level of service. It was simply the Ritz way of serving a customer—any customer.

What the server didn't know was that the person requesting the water was in fact the president and CEO of the company delivering supplies to the hotel. He made a habit of riding along with his delivery truck drivers from time to time, just to stay in touch with employees and customers.

Of course, the actions of the Ritz-Carlton employee on the loading dock of the hotel taught the owner of the restaurant supply company a valuable lesson about the value of values.

You Won't Need Many (Core) Values

In *Built to Last*, Collins and Porras speak specifically about an organization's core values. Individually or organizationally, we only need a few *core values* to guide and govern our behavior. In fact, too many will dilute their power and diminish desired behavior.

Choose your values carefully, because they'll be the tools you use to drive your decisions on a daily basis. Your values *must be seen* to be real. If you say, for example, that one of your core values is integrity, then integrity must become a visible behavior in everything you do.

> *Choose your values carefully, because they'll be the tools you use to drive your decisions on a daily basis.*

The value of values, not unlike vision and mission, is that when clearly defined, they provide the clarity and focus you'll need for sustained improvement and productivity—just like those enduring companies described in *Built to Last*.

Now It's Your Turn

1. Take a blank piece of paper or fire up your word processor and create two columns. In the left column, list four or five values that are at your or your organization's core. In the right column, describe the behavior(s) associated with the value on the left.

2. By the way, if you choose the value of integrity, and almost everyone does, I would suggest this value has a much deeper meaning than just being honest. It describes a moral soundness that pervades

every action of an individual or organization. In this context, time management, for example, becomes an opportunity to display integrity.

3. After the list of core values is created, think deeply about each of them and be certain you intend to commit to living out these values on a day-to-day basis, personally and corporately.

More Thoughts on the Value of Values

"Set your expectations high; find men and women whose integrity and values you respect; get their agreement on a course of action; and give them your ultimate trust."
—John Fellows Akers

"Authentic values are those by which a life can be lived, which can form a people that produces great deeds and thoughts."
—Allan Bloom

"Success is knowing what your values are and living in a way consistent with your values."
—Danny Cox

"Try not to become a man of success, but rather a man of value."
—Albert Einstein

"What you do speaks so loudly I can't hear what you say."
—Ralph Waldo Emerson

"Values are not trendy items that are casually traded in."
—Ellen Goodman

"Beauty, truth, friendship, love, creation—these are the great values of life. We can't prove them, or explain them, yet they are the most stable things in our lives."
—Jesse Herman Holmes

"Get a right idea of values. Material possessions that you do not need and cannot use may be only an encumbrance. Let your guiding rule be not how much but how good."

—Grenville Kleiser

"We shall be rich or poor only as we seek or reject those values which make us so."
—Elmer G. Leterman

"Happiness is that state of consciousness which proceeds from the achievement of one's values."
—Ayn Rand

"Conscience is the voice of values long and deeply infused into one's sinews and blood."
—Elliot L. Richardson

"The major value in life is not what you get. The major value in life is what you become."
—Jim Rohn

"Values are principles and ideas that bring meaning to the seemingly mundane experience of life. A meaningful life that ultimately brings happiness and pride requires you to respond to temptations as well as challenges with honor, dignity, and courage."
—Laura Schlessinger

"Life's up and downs provide windows of opportunity to determine your values and goals. Think of using all obstacles as stepping stones to build the life you want."
—Marsha Sinetar

"Ethical behavior is concerned above all with human values, not with legalisms."
—A.M. Sullivan

CHAPTER 8

✦

Leaders with Perspective Have Followers

"It's a terrible thing to look over
your shoulder when you are trying
to lead—and find no one there."
~ Franklin D. Roosevelt

Are leaders made or are leaders born? I'm often asked that question by clients or at speaking engagements. My answer is always the same, "Yes." Some men and women are born with leadership ability. For as long as they can remember, they have had the ability to cause people to want to follow them.

However, leadership skills and abilities can be taught and enhanced. Just look at any of our military academies, for example. They take young men and women who have proven leadership ability and begin to elevate those skills to new levels.

> *Why do leaders have followers? Because they're able to demonstrate that they know where they're going.*

Why do leaders have followers? Because they're able to demonstrate that they know where they're going, why they're headed in a particular direction, and they model behaviors conducive to their vision and mission. They have perspective.

Peter Drucker on Leadership

Peter Drucker is one of my true heroes for a number of reasons, not the least of which was his clear understanding of the differences and the similarities of leaders and managers. While both roles are incredibly important to any organization, their roles are different. We'll discuss those differences in chapter 20.

In an excerpt from the book, *The Daily Drucker*, we find a classic understanding of what a real leader looks like.

The leader who basically focuses on himself or herself is going to mislead. The three most charismatic leaders in this century inflicted more suffering on the human race than almost any other trio in history. Hitler, Stalin, and Mao. What matters is not the leader's charisma. For leadership is not magnetic personality—that can just as well be demagoguery. It is not "making friends and influencing people"—that is flattery.

Leadership is the lifting of a man's vision to higher sights, the raising of a man's performance to a higher standard, the building of a man's personality beyond its normal limitations. Nothing better prepares the ground for such leadership than a spirit of management that confirms in the day-to-day practices of the organization strict principles of conduct and responsibility, high standards of performance, and respect for the individual and his work.

Peter Drucker has it exactly right; leaders share their vision, they help their followers see what they see. Leaders raise performance levels by answering the "why" questions, and they inspire responsibility by clarifying core values.

Developing perspective is the role of every leader in every organization.

Is Anyone Following?

If you're in a position of leadership, personally or professionally, you have to look over your shoulder every now and then to see if anyone is following you. If not, then you're either not a leader, or you haven't demonstrated that you know where you're going and why.

The Bible says, "without a vision people perish." I think the one thing that separates true leaders from those who what to be, or think they are, is vision. More specifically, it's perspective.

Leaders know where they're going, or what they want to accomplish; they know why, and their behavior validates their intentions.

Leaders know where they're going, or what they want to accomplish; they know why, and their behavior validates their intentions.

Now It's Your Turn

How would you rate your leadership quotient?

1. Do you have a clear vision for where you want to go or what you want to accomplish?

2. Is your vision clearly defined?

3. Do you have followers? If not, do you know why no one is choosing to follow you?

4. Write the name of the person you consider a true leader. How did that individual earn that distinction with you?

In the chapters that follow, you'll take your dream of what could be and develop the plans, goals, and actions to bring your vision to reality.

More Thoughts on Leadership

"The true leader inspires in others self trust, guiding their eyes to the spirit, the goal."
—Amos Bronson Alcott

"The first job of a leader is to define a vision for the organization…but without longevity of leadership, you can have the 'vision of the month club.'"
—Warren G. Bennis

"Leadership is much more an art, a belief, a condition of the heart, than a set of things to do. The visible signs of artful leadership are expressed, ultimately, in its practice."
—Max DePree

"Though leadership may be hard to define, the one characteristic common to all leaders is the ability to make things happen."
—Ted W. Engstrom

"Leaders come in many forms, with many styles and diverse qualities. There are quiet leaders and leaders one can hear in the next county. Some find strength in eloquence, some in judgment, some in courage."

—John W. Gardner

"Leadership is achieved by ability, alertness, experience and keeping posted; by willingness to accept responsibility; a knack for getting along with people; an open mind and a head that stays clear under stress."

—E.F. Girard

"The very essence of leadership is that you have to have a vision. It's got to be a vision you articulate clearly and forcefully on every occasion. You can't blow an uncertain trumpet."

—Theodore M. Hesburgh

"Of a good leader, who talks little, when his work is done, his aim fulfilled, they will say, 'We did this ourselves.'"

—Lao-Tzu

"Leaders aren't born, they are made. And they are made just like anything else, through hard work. And that's the price we'll have to pay to achieve that goal, or any goal."

—Vince Lombardi

"Be like jockey Willie Shoemaker. He's the best in the business because he has the lightest touch on the reins. They say the horse never knows he's there—unless he's needed."

—Harvey Mackay

"Leadership is action, not position."

—Donald H. McGannon

"Be willing to make decisions. That's the most important quality of a good leader. Don't fall victim to what I call the ready-aim-aim-aim syndrome. You must be willing to fire."

—T. Boone Pickens

Section Three: Purposeful Performance

CHAPTER 9

Defining Performance

Performance is your reality.
Forget everything else.
~ Harold S. Geneen

Defining performance is the second piece of our three-piece process for moving from activity to achievement. In this section, we'll describe how your vision becomes a reality. Performance is all about making it happen—whatever "it" may be.

In order to link your performance with your perspective, you'll need to develop plans, set goals, and make strategic decisions about what actions to take and when.

Strategy

Planning is essential for improving performance and production. You can try to get along without a plan, but what you'll end up with is nothing more than random acts of progress—a herky-jerky success pattern that is short-term and discouraging.

In a recent article in *Success* magazine, titled "Five Vital Signs to Monitor and Improve the Health of Your Business," Rhonda Abrams, owner of The Planning Shop, is quoted as saying, "Many, many small-business people and entrepreneurs are very busy, but they're not necessarily making progress." She went on to say, "You want to make sure you're moving forward and the only way to do that is with a (business) plan."

Author after author and expert after expert in the field of business and personal development make the same claim; planning is essential to business or personal success.

Goals

Without goals, your plans stand little or no chance of being completed. The fact is that there is no substitute for goal setting and there is no sustained progress either. You'll simply become a slave to the pressing and the proximate. You'll succumb to the crisis of the day, or crisis of the moment, and no real progress will be made.

Those same experts that laud the power of a plan would also say goals are absolutely essential to success and achievement.

Actions

When we talk about actions as the sixth step in our process for improvement, we're not just talking about being busy. We're talking about doing those things that will have the highest payoff in terms of your strategy and your goals.

If your actions are in alignment with your plans and goals, you'll make phenomenal progress. If your actions are subject to the pressing and the proximate, you'll make no real progress at all, but you'll be busy!

If your actions are in alignment with your plans and goals, you'll make phenomenal progress.

As we drill down on the issue of defining performance, we'll look specifically at the practical side of moving from activity to achievement.

We built the foundation for moving from activity to achievement by clarifying our perspective. We now have a vision statement that will provide the focus we need to move in a specific direction. We have a written mission statement that explains why we're doing what we're doing, and we've selected three to five core values to drive our behavior.

As we drill down on the issue of defining performance, we'll look specifically at the practical side of moving from activity to achievement.

Now we start to put skin on the skeleton of performance improvement by developing strategies, setting goals, and taking specific actions to guarantee our success.

So roll up your sleeves and put on your thinking cap. It's time to define performance and increase productivity.

Let's get to work!

More Thoughts on Defining Performance

"In business, excellence of performance manifests itself, among other things, in the advancing of methods and processes; in the improvement of products, in more perfect organization ... and in the establishment of right relations with customers and with the community."
—Louis D. Brandeis

"What you want to do, you do. The rest is just talk."
—John Cleek

"The way to get started is to quit talking and begin doing."
—Walt Disney

"You can either take action, or you can hang back and hope for a miracle. Miracles are great, but they are so unpredictable."
—Peter F. Drucker

"Conditions are never just right. People who delay action until all factors are favorable do nothing."
—William Feather

"Resolve to perform what you ought. Perform without fail what you resolve."
—Benjamin Franklin

"The best way to inspire people to superior performance is to convince them by everything you do and by your everyday attitude that you are wholeheartedly supporting them."
—Harold S. Geneen

"Why wait? Life is not a dress rehearsal. Quit practicing what you are going to do, and just do it."
—Marilyn Grey

"Even when you're on the right track, you'll get run over if you just sit there."
—Will Rogers

"Your performance depends on your people. Select the best, train them, and back them."

—Donald Rumsfeld

"You cannot cross the sea merely by standing and staring at the water."

—Rabindranath Tagore

CHAPTER 10

※

The Need for Strategic Thinking and Planning

*What business strategy is all about;
what distinguishes it from all other kinds
of business planning—is, in a word,
competitive advantage.*
~ Keniche Ohnae

We live in a very situational environment, individually and organizationally. We expect quick service, quick delivery, and rapid responses. We don't think we have time to wait and we mistakenly decide we don't have time to plan.

Recent surveys indicate that an alarming number of small businesses have neither a business plan nor a strategic plan to guide their daily actions.

Recent surveys indicate that an alarming number of small businesses have neither a business plan nor a strategic plan to guide their daily actions. If you asked these small business owners why they don't have such a plan, they would more than likely say they're too busy to write one. I don't need to tell you what the failure rate is for small business across the country. Do you see a pattern developing here?

I suspect the statistics for personal strategic planning would be equally low and the consequences just as disturbing. How many baby boomers standing at the door of retirement today have been following a financial plan that has them ready to walk away from businesses or careers and enjoy their golden years? Right. Not many.

The Missing Link

Strategic thinking is the missing link between an individual or an organizational vision for a preferred future, and making the vision a reality.

Both vision casting and strategic planning are admittedly intuitive. In both instances, we're looking into the future and seeing what could or should be, but that's the way of change. Look around the room you're in right now. Everything you can see or touch was, at one time, nothing more than an idea in someone's mind. First came the vision of what could be, then came the product. But, we must connect the dots between the vision of what we want to achieve and the actual product. That connection results from strategic thinking and planning.

It Isn't Brain Surgery, It's Planning

Developing strategy is simply the first step of a three-step process for achieving what we want to achieve. Improving performance or increasing productivity will result from developing strategies (plans) that will frame goals and focus activity.

Strategy + Measurable Objectives + Actions = Preferred Change

This simple formula can create phenomenal change in the life of an individual or an organization. There are just three pieces to this little puzzle and, when they're connected, you'll have a clear understanding of what you want to accomplish, what you'll need to measure along the way, and the specific work that has to be done to make it happen.

It's one thing to have a vision; it's quite another thing to make the vision a reality. Visions are a dime a dozen. Everyone has a vision for something better. Very few individuals or organizations have a specific plan for converting their dream to reality.

Strategic thinking is necessary, precisely because it forces us to look beyond the present and, specifically, beyond the current crisis. Strategic thinking is important because:

> *It's one thing to have a vision; it's quite another thing to make the vision a reality. Visions are a dime a dozen. Everyone has a vision for something better. Very few individuals or organizations have a specific plan for converting their dream to reality.*

1. It serves as the arbiter for our decision making. It provides the perspective we need to make good decisions.

2. Based on our vision, mission and values, we have context for why we're doing what we're doing.

3. It serves as a beacon; warning us when we're in danger of drifting off course.

4. It helps us make principle-based decisions.

Without strategic thinking, unpredictable circumstances and day-to-day challenges would cause us to lose track of our overarching purpose.

In this section, we begin the process of linking our vision with the strategy, objectives, and actions necessary to produce the desired results.

Don't underestimate the importance of planning as an essential element for moving from activity to achievement.

More Thoughts on Strategic Thinking

"It is much less what we do than what we think that fits us for the future."
—Philip J. Bailey

"Concentrate all your thoughts upon the work at hand. The sun's rays do not burn until brought to a focus."
—Alexander Graham Bell

"Thought is the seat of action. The ancestor of every action is thought."
—Ralph Waldo Emerson

"Great thoughts converted to practice will become great accomplishments."
—William Hazlitt

"Thought precedes action as lightning does thunder."
—Heinrich Heine

"If you are to step out into the unknown, the place to begin is with the exploration of the inner territory."
—James Kouzes and Barry Posner

"The task is not so much to see what no one yet has seen, but to think what nobody yet has thought about that which everybody sees."
—Arthur Schopenhauer

"Thought is the strongest thing we have. Work done by true and profound thought—that is real force."

—Albert Schweitzer

"Thinking is the place where intelligent actions begin. We pause long enough to look more carefully at a situation, to see more of its character, to think about why it's happening, to notice how it's affecting us and others."

—Margaret J. Wheatley

"Are you willing to think? Consider carefully, for the answer to that question will largely determine your success or failure in life. The functions of your mind, no less than the muscles of your body, receive their strength through repeated use."

—John M. Wilson

CHAPTER 11

Developing Strategies 101

You can have anything you want—
if you want it badly enough.
You can be anything you want to be,
do anything you set out to accomplish
if you hold to that desire with singleness of purpose.
~ Abraham Lincoln

Because strategy is the first step in bringing about the preferred changes seen in our vision, it's useful to discuss how to develop a strategy statement. The process I recommend for creating a strategy statement is a two-step methodology: develop strategic categories based on the vision, and write a single strategic statement of what you want to accomplish in the specific category.

Strategic Categories

Individual strategic categories might include:

- Income

- Education

- Career Development

- Relationship Building

- Health

- Nutrition

Organizational categories might include:

- Sales

- Marketing

- Organizational Development

- Personnel Development

- Training

- Process Improvement

Strategy Statements

A strategy differs from an objective in that strategies do not have to be measurable. A strategy may be quantifiable, but it doesn't have to be. Breaking out the strategy into measurable objectives will handle the quantification issue.

> *A strategy differs from an objective in that strategies do not have to be measurable.*

On an individual level, one might have a strategy to improve his or her education, or to lose weight, or to seek a management position or promotion.

Organizational strategy statements tend to be more quantitative than individual statements. For example, an organization may have a strategy for increasing sales by X percent in a given fiscal or calendar year.

Examples of an individual strategy statement might be:

- "Become a project manager in XYZ division by the end of this year."

- "Improve my health through nutrition and exercise."

Examples of an organizational strategy statement might be:

- "Develop a marketing plan for 2009."

- "Increase pretax profits by 5 percent company-wide in 2010."

The strategy statement zeros in on a specific category, in which you will then set measurable objectives and take specific actions.

The Power of a Plan

Wishing or hoping or wanting something to be different will not result in change. Wishing, hoping, or wanting, without planning and action, produces nothing but disappointment.

Developing strategies is the first step in ensuring that we'll see the change we desire manifested in specific behavior. Improving performance, productivity, and profitability starts with clarifying what we want. From there, we can set goals and take meaningful action.

As you'll see in the next chapter, developing plans means changing the status quo, and that makes people very uncomfortable.

Instead of climbing out of the ruts we find ourselves in, we'd rather decorate!

Developing strategies is the first step in ensuring that we'll see the change we desire manifested in specific behavior.

Develop Your Success Strategies

Create three personal strategic categories you want to see improvement in:

1.

2.

3

Develop three organizational strategies for improved performance and productivity:

1.

2.

3.

More Thoughts on Planning

"If you board the wrong train, it is no use running along the corridor in the other direction."

—Dietrich Bonhoeffer

"While it is well enough to leave footprints on the sands of time, it is even more important to make sure they point in a commendable direction."

—James Branch Cabell

"You've removed most of the roadblocks to success when you've learned the difference between motion and direction."

—Bill Copeland

"I find the great thing in this world is not so much where we stand, as in what direction we are moving. To reach the port of heaven, we must sail sometimes with the wind and sometimes against it—but we must sail, and not drift, nor lie at anchor."

—Oliver Wendell Holmes

"I am here for a purpose and that purpose is to grow into a mountain, not to shrink to a grain of sand. Henceforth will I apply ALL my efforts to become the highest mountain of all and I will strain my potential until it cries for mercy."

—Og Mandino

"Determine what specific goal you want to achieve. Then dedicate yourself to its attainment with unswerving singleness of purpose, the trenchant zeal of a crusader."

—Paul J. Meyer

"Singleness of purpose is one of the chief essentials for success in life, no matter what may be one's aim."

—John D. Rockefeller

"Every life should have a purpose to which it can give the energies of its mind and the enthusiasms of its heart."

—C. Neil Strait

"If one advances confidently in the direction of his dreams, and endeavors to live the life which he has imagined, he will meet with a success unexpected in common hours."

—Henry David Thoreau

CHAPTER 12

The Challenge of Change

Without change there is no innovation,
creativity, or incentive for improvement.
Those who initiate change will have a better opportunity
to manage the change that is inevitable.
~ William Pollard

Remember that a strategy is a plan for preferred change. The whole idea behind creating a strategy is to change the way things are now.

That being the case, changing the status quo will usually involve:

- *Starting* something that doesn't currently exist.

- *Stopping* something that does exist but isn't particularly effective.

- *Doing more of* something in order to get the results we want.

- *Doing less* of something that isn't getting the desired results.

And, herein lies the problem.

Creatures of Habit

Changing the way things are, even when we're not getting the results we want, creates a great deal of anxiety. Why? Because most of what we do, we do because of habit.

Humans are, if nothing else, creatures of habit. Most of what we do isn't based on policy, procedure, peer pressure, or because mother told us to. We do what we do because of habit.

Studies have shown that as much as 80 percent of our daily activity is based on habit. The same is true for the choices we make each day. Choices are made in five ways:

- Spur of the moment

- Consciously

- Pressure from others

- Habit

- Default (because we have to)

> **Studies have shown that as much as 80 percent of our daily activity is based on habit.**

By far and away, the primary determiner of the choices we make is *habit.*

Why We Don't Want to Change

Here are some facts about change you'll need to know in order to cope with the natural resistance to change:

- Most people will change only *if the alternative is worse* than the change itself.

- People want *stability* in the midst of change.

- For change to be successful, it must be *planned.*

- Changing behavior will mean changing *habits.*

> **I find it fascinating that most of us will only consider making significant change is we think the alternative is worse.**

I find it fascinating that most of us will only consider making significant change if we think the alternative is worse. Evidently, changing for the sake of improving takes a back seat to the fear that things *might* be worse if we change the way things are now.

People do want *stability* in the midst of change. This is why managers and business owners must do a fair amount of hand-holding in explaining the need for specific changes.

One of the ways managers and owners can provide the desired stability people want is by clearly showing there's a *plan* in place for making the necessary changes. This will help those affected by the change to understand the thinking behind it. Open communication will go a long way in alleviating the anxiety that change brings about.

Old habits die hard. Understanding this, however, is a key success factor in changing the status quo. Remember also there will be no improvement or achievement without change.

Challenge Yourself to Change

Make a list of five things you need to change in order to create a different reality than you're experiencing now.

1.

2.

3.

4.

5.

More Thoughts on the Value of Change

"Change is a process and not a destination, it never ends!"
—James Belasco

"We must all obey the great law of change. It is the most powerful law of nature."
—Edmund Burke

"Little men with little minds and little imagination jog through life in little ruts, smugly resisting all changes which would jar their little worlds."
—Marie Fraser

"You never change things by fighting the existing reality. To change something, build a new model that makes the existing model obsolete."
—Buckminster Fuller

"Blessed is the man who has discovered that there is nothing permanent in life but change."

—A.P. Gouthey

"I cannot say whether things will get better if we change; what I can say is they must change if they are to get better."

—Georg Christopher Lichtenberg

"Welcome change as a friend; try to visualize new possibilities and the blessings it is bound to bring you. Never stop learning and never stop growing; that is the key to a rich and fascinating life."

—Alexander de Seversky

"Progress is impossible without change; and those who cannot change their minds cannot change anything."

—George Bernard Shaw

"Change is the process by which the future invades our lives."

—Alvin Toffler

"View change as the one constant in your life. Welcome it. Expect it. Anticipate it."

—Denis Waitley

"Change is the watchword of progression. When we tire of well-worn ways, we seek for new. This restless craving in the souls of men spurs them to climb, and to seek the mountain view."

—Ella Wheeler Wilcox

CHAPTER 13

There's Gold in Your Goals

Desire is the key to motivation, but it's determination and commitment to an unrelenting pursuit of your goal—a commitment to excellence—that will enable you to attain the success you seek.
~ Mario Andretti

If strategy is the catalyst for change, then goals are the fuel. When it comes to moving from activity to achievement, your success or failure will be determined by how seriously you take goal setting.

I never cease to be amazed at how virtually everyone agrees on the value of goal setting but, year in and year out, statistics show that fewer than 5 percent of individuals or organizations have written goals to guide their activities.

Goals provide clarity and focus for our daily, weekly, and monthly actions.

Goals direct activity. They provide the criteria by which we monitor progress. Goals provide clarity and focus for our daily, weekly, and monthly actions.

If we understand that we'd make more progress by setting goals, then why don't we?

Here are five reasons we don't set goals:

1. **Procrastination.** Choosing not to choose. Procrastination is nothing more than *a bad habit* and one that must be broken in order for performance to improve and production increase.

2. **Fear of Failure.** We don't set goals because we don't believe we can achieve them. *Past failures* limit future victories. We may have tried setting goals before and didn't achieve them, so we just don't do it anymore. Bad plan!

3. **Lack of Commitment.** Achievement is about doing, not about dreaming, or wishing, or hoping. No achievement of any kind is possible without *doing unpleasant or difficult things.* Goals, taken seriously, help motivate us to get the job done.

4. **Lack of Responsibility.** Not taking personal responsibility for our own success and achievement. We convince ourselves that *someone else* is going to ride in on the white horse and take over where we failed to act. Again, bad plan. No one will, and no one else should, take responsibility for our success and personal development.

5. **Lack of Faith.** We simply don't believe, deep inside, that we can perform at a higher level. We may have a personal history of average performance and limited accomplishments, and simply lack the self-belief in our ability to be to any more successful than we already are.

Regardless of the reasons for not setting goals, the fact remains that the rich treasures of life, and of success and achievement, will *not* come to us unless goals are set and met. It's that simple.

> *The rich treasures of life, and of success and achievement, will not come to us unless goals are set and met. It's that simple.*

Six Goals for Your Goals

Our goals must be *aligned with our strategy.* After we've clarified our vision, developed strategic categories, and written strategic statements, it's time to set goals.

Our goals must be *realistic.* If a goal is unattainable, our subconscious mind will not accept it as doable and this will quickly lead to giving up.

Each goal must be *time sensitive.* We must have a starting point and a finish line. How much? By when? These are the two questions every goal must be able to answer.

Here are six goals for your goals:

1. **See the Goal as a Reality.** Remember the value of vision. As Stephen Covey suggests, "Begin with the end in mind." See what you want to accomplish *as if* it were finished, and begin to act as if your goal was a done deal.

2. **Identify the Obstacles.** You know there are going to be obstacles or difficulties in achieving your goal, so deal with them up front.

Obstacles can be people, locations, systems, structures, or money. It doesn't matter. What does matter is that you intellectually acknowledge they exist and that you're prepared to deal with them.

3. **See the Benefits**. You've done the hard work of developing strategies based on your vision. You've listed the obstacles you'll have to face and overcome. Now it's time to see the benefits you'll enjoy after reaching your goal. Write those benefits down—right beside the goal itself. Seeing the benefits becomes a real motivator to accomplish your goal.

4. **Commit to a Plan of Action**. Remember what we said earlier, *achievement is about doing*, not about dreaming. Take a large goal and break it down into bite-sized pieces. Slice the elephant into small fillets and dig in!

5. **Be Flexible**. *Things change*. Expect the unexpected. You know that no matter how meticulously you plan things, stuff happens that will throw you off track. Get back on track as soon as possible and keep focused on the finish line. By the way, a strong commitment to achieving your goal will help you make those necessary course adjustments.

6. **Enjoy the Journey**. Moving from activity to achievement is a journey, not a race. We didn't get the way we are overnight, and we aren't going to change things for the better overnight either. Enjoy the ups and downs. Accept them as *character builders*.

There you have it—the condensed version for why goal setting is so necessary for achievement of any kind. We could have tried to make each point a stand-alone chapter, but why bother? You don't have to be taught about the importance of goal setting as much as you need to be reminded. It's not a matter of knowing, it's a matter of doing.

More Thoughts on Goals

"The purpose of setting goals is to inspire action, not predict it."

—John H. Clark

"An oxcart is as useless to a man as a rocket ship if he does not know where he wants to go."

—Johann von Goethe

"In the absence of clearly-defined goals, we become strangely loyal to performing daily trivia until ultimately we become enslaved by it."

—Robert A. Heinlein

"Know what you want to do, hold the thought firmly, and do every day what should be done, and every sunset will see you that much nearer to your goal."

—Elbert Hubbard

"The man with average mentality, but with control, a definite goal and a clear conception of how it can be gained and, above all, with the power of application and labor, wins in the end."

—William Howard Taft

CHAPTER 14

※

Goal Setting Made Easy

The value of the goal lies in the goal itself;
and therefore the goal cannot be attained
unless it is pursued for its own sake.
~ Arnold J. Toynbee

I've made the case for the importance of goal setting and why most people don't set goals. Now it's time to take all the information we already know to be true about goals and set some of our own.

Before we do, though, it might be helpful to engage in a little due diligence as it relates to goal setting. A good place to begin would be to define a goal.

A goal is a measurable objective which is to be achieved in a specific time frame.

You're probably familiar with the acronym SMART when referring to goals, but a reminder of what it stands for might be helpful. SMART goals are:

- Specific

- Measurable

- Aligned with Strategy

- Realistic

- Time Sensitive

I mentioned in an earlier chapter that the primary difference between a strategy and a goal is that goals must be measurable, strategies do not.

The power of the goal lies in its specificity. When we write out a specific objective, in quantifiable terms, we answer those two all important questions: How much? By when?

A well-written goal leaves nothing to the imagination. An unmeasurable goal is nothing more than a wish or a dream.

Note the difference:

- Unmeasurable goal: *Be productive today.*

- SMART goal: *Mail out three speaker packets to clients X, Y,and Z by 5:00 PM today.*

> *A well-written goal leaves nothing to the imagination.*

The Benefits of Goal Setting

Here are several benefits, individually or organizationally, for setting goals:

1. Goals clarify what we want to accomplish.

2. Goals identify the results we want to achieve.

3. Goals enable us to measure our progress.

4. Goals create a sense of accomplishment.

5. Goals provide the ladder we need to get out of a rut.

It doesn't get any better than that for generating the confidence we need to improve our position, individually and/or organizationally.

I'm often asked in interviews or workshops why people and organizations don't accomplish more than they do. My answer is always the same; lack of purpose and lack of clarity.

> *Success and achievement result from having a clear vision and a cogent plan for bringing the vision to reality.*

When we develop perspective, we clarify our purpose. When we develop strategy and set goals, we establish the focus and clarity we need to make the improvements we want to make, personally or organizationally.

Success and achievement are not the result of haphazard actions or the luck of the draw. Success and achievement result from having a clear vision and a cogent plan for bringing the vision to reality.

Climbing a Mountain

In a 2008 article in the *Wall Street Journal*, executive coach and mountain climber David Lin drew a correlation between running a company and setting goals. During the interview, he said, "In the context of mountain climbing, all team members have to be engaged in the process months before the climb ... testing equipment, suggesting routes, collectively deciding on rules to obey on the mountain. If everyone isn't on the same page before the climb, we won't be when we're on the mountain, which can be disastrous. The same applies to reaching business goals."

Charting a Ship's Course

In the mid 1960s, I spent four years in the United States Navy, serving as a navigator's assistant. During that time, I learned the fundamental principles of navigation, which I would later apply to personal performance improvement.

Those fundamental navigational principles enabled my shipmates and me to chart a course that took our ship from San Diego, California to the South China Sea.

I think you'll recognize the similarities between the process of charting a course and moving from activity to achievement.

The fundamental principals of navigation are:

- **Look Ahead.** Determine your destination.

- **Look Around.** Get your bearings.

- **Chart the Course.** Develop a plan.

- **Set the Sails.** Execute the plan.

- **Adjust the Course.** Evaluate progress.

Whether climbing a mountain or charting a ship's course, the message is the same; have a plan and set objectives. Why should we think improving our performance and productivity would be any different?

Now It's Your Turn

Set two SMART personal goals and then two goals to move you further ahead in your career.

Personal Goals: (Remember: How much? By when?)

1.

2.

Career Goals:

1.

2.

More Thoughts on Goal Setting

"A man without a purpose is like a ship without a rudder, a waif, a nothing, a no man. Have a purpose in life, and, having it, throw such strength and muscle into your work as God has given you."
—Thomas Carlyle

"The establishment of a goal is the key to successful living."
—Dr. Ari Kiev

"Keep a definite goal of achievement constantly in view. Realize that work well and worthily done makes life truly worth living."
—Grenville Kleiser

"Write out your goal. What are the obstacles? What are the rewards? Is it worth it? Are you willing to pay the price? If so, visualize the rewards and get excited about it. Keep reselling yourself! Go forward!"
—Maxwell Maltz

"Have the dogged determination to follow through to achieve your goal; regardless of circumstances or whatever other people say, think, or do."
—Paul J. Meyer

"You have a rudder-like control on your life, and you get that control largely by the goals you set with deep desire."
—Earl Nightingale

"Let me tell you the secret that has led me to my goal. My strength lies solely in my tenacity."

—Louis Pasteur

"My philosophy of life is that if we make up our mind what we are going to make of our lives, then work hard toward that goal, we never lose—somehow we win out."

—Ronald Reagan

"Any man who selects a goal in life which can be fully achieved has already defined his own limitations."

—Cavett Robert

"Reality forms around your commitments. The achievement of your goal is assured the moment you commit yourself to it."

—Max Steingart

"The most important key to achieving great success is to decide upon your goal and launch, get started, take action, move."

—John Wooden

"Without organization and leadership towards a realistic goal, there is no chance of realizing more than a small percentage of your potential."

—John Wooden

"If you can't picture your goal, you won't have the courage to start. Your imagination is working with you or against you every minute of every hour of every week of every year of your life."

—A.B. ZuTavern

CHAPTER 15

The Fear of Failure

Never let the fear of failure be an excuse for not trying.
Society tells us that to fail is the most terrible thing in the world,
but I know it isn't. Failure is a part of what makes us human.
~ Amber Deckers

If we conducted a survey of what men and women most fear, we'd get a list of the usual suspects: the fear of speaking in public, the fear of death, the fear of rejection. But on that list, and probably among the top five answers, would be the fear of failure.

Interestingly, fear of failure is also one of the chief reasons people, and many organizations, don't set goals. They're afraid they won't, or can't, accomplish their goals.

This an interesting phenomenon, considering we live in a time when innovation, creativity, and being on the cutting edge are on the lips of almost every manager and every organization on the planet. It's an interesting paradox; we want innovation, we encourage risk taking but, on an individual level at least, we're scared to death of failure.

Failure Isn't Rewarded

In my opinion, the fact that failure isn't rewarded in corporate America is a colossal mistake.

Do you know anybody who has received an award or recognition for failing? "Good effort, Simpson, your attempt to develop the high compression dipstick failed miserably, but here's a check for $1,000 for giving it the old college try." I don't think so.

In my opinion, the fact that failure isn't rewarded in corporate America is a colossal mistake.

Let me ask you a question. Haven't the greatest lessons of your life come from your failures, not from your successes?

Don't we learn as much from what didn't work as we do from what did? Failure is a fabulous teacher. Now, having said that, I'm not encouraging you to get out there and fail, but I am saying you should put failure in perspective and let it teach you.

Thomas Edison on Failure

Thomas Edison is credited with creating the incandescent light bulb. It's reported that he conducted more than ten thousand experiments before he found success. As the story goes, during the course of his attempts to develop the light bulb, he was contacted by a reporter who wanted to interview him about the new invention he was working on.

As the interview began, the young reporter asked Edison why he continued to experiment with this thing called a light bulb, when he had already failed more than five thousand times to reach his goal.

Edison answered by suggesting that he hadn't failed five thousand times. He had merely discovered five thousand ways it didn't work, and he would continue experimenting until he found out what did. What a novel idea—seeing failed experiments as opportunities to learn, instead of reasons to quit.

Let Life Teach You

Jim Rohn, perhaps America's foremost business philosopher, has encouraged his audiences for decades to "let life teach you." This great motivator is simply stating what every one of us knows to be true. The great lessons of life come from what doesn't work, at least as much as from what does.

The great lessons of life come from what doesn't work, at least as much as from what does.

Failure and Goal Setting

I stated in chapter 13 that strategies are the catalyst for change but goals are the fuel. Goals provide clarity and focus for what we want to accomplish.

Will our goals always be met? Will we always succeed because we've established goals? Clearly not, but if we learn from what didn't work, make necessary adjustments and keep moving forward, we'll succeed far more often than we'll fail.

Insights on Failure

Here a few facts about failure you might find helpful:

- Failure teaches us the lessons we need to succeed.

- Failure fuels progress *if* we learn from what doesn't work.

- All great men and women develop the habit of confronting their fear of failure.

- We overcome our fear of failure through perseverance.

- Failure is never final.

Goal setting is the key to moving from activity to achievement. Failure is just a part of the goal setting process. Success never lasts and failure isn't fatal.

Set your goals with your eyes wide open. You may not achieve what you want to achieve in the time frames you've established. So what? Make the necessary adjustments and move on. Learn from what didn't work, fix what you can, and accept the things you can't. But never stop setting those all-important goals that will fuel the success and achievement you know you can reach, if you keep trying.

Facing Your Fear

List three great lessons you've learned from past failures or mistakes.

1.

2.

3.

What fear of failure are you facing right now that must be dealt with?

What are you going to do to confront this fear?

Whose help do you need?

More Thoughts on Failure

"No matter how hard you work for success, if your thought is saturated with fear of failure, it will kill your efforts, neutralize your endeavors, and make success impossible."
—Charles Baudouin

"If you are frightened and look for failure and poverty, you will get them, no matter how hard you try to succeed. Lack of faith in yourself, if what life will do for you, cuts you off from the good things of the world. Expect victory and you make victory."
—Preston Bradley

"Those who try and fail are much wiser than those who never try for fear of failure."
—André Bustanoby

"Develop success from failures. Discouragement and failure are two of the surest stepping stones to success."
—Dale Carnegie

"Many of life's failures are people who did not realize how close they were to success when they gave up."
—Thomas Edison

"One who fears failure limits his activities. Failure is only the opportunity more intelligently to begin again."
—Henry Ford

"We are neurotically haunted today by the imminence, and by the ignominy, of failure. We know at how frightening a cost one succeeds; to fail is something too awful to think about."
—Louis Kronenberger

"Remind thyself, in the darkest moments, that every failure is only a step toward success."
—Og Mandino

"Far better it is to dare mighty things, to win glorious triumphs even though checkered by failure, than to take rank with those poor spirits who neither enjoy much nor suffer much, because they live in the gray twilight that knows neither victory nor defeat."

—Theodore Roosevelt

"Failure is as much a part of life as success is and by no means something in front of which one sits down and howls as though it is a scandal and a shame."

—J. Neville Ward

CHAPTER 16

❖

Taking Action

"The way to get started is to quit talking and begin doing."
~ Walt Disney

Here's where the rubber meets the road when it comes to moving from activity to achievement. Taking personal initiative and doing those things that need to be done are the keys to success and achievement in any endeavor.

We can have the vision for what we want to accomplish crystal clear in our mind's eye. We may have developed elaborate plans and set meaningful goals but, if we fail to execute, if we fail to take the appropriate action at the appropriate time, it will all be for naught. Achievement is about doing, not dreaming. Success is 10 percent vision and 90 percent execution.

Achievement is about doing, not dreaming. Success is 10 percent vision and 90 percent execution.

Taking the appropriate action at the appropriate time has so many benefits. Here are just a few:

- Action brings learning and growth.

- Action leads to solutions.

- Action takes courage.

- Action builds confidence.

When we take the necessary action, we inevitably learn and grow from the experience. Experience is a great teacher. Even negative experiences are chock-full of teachable moments. Remember, good judgment often comes from bad experiences.

Action leads to solutions. By taking action, we often find solutions for problems we didn't even know we had. Stories abound of new services discovered and new products developed as a result of trying to accomplish something different than what actually emerged.

One of the reasons we don't take action when we should is because of fear. Real or imagined, fear will often prevent us from taking the action necessary to achieve the results we desire. Taking action often means summoning up the courage we need to keep moving forward.

By taking action, we often find solutions for problems we didn't even know we had.

Lastly, action builds confidence. Even if we don't get the exact results we want, and especially if we had to step out in faith and courage, we develop the confidence we need to keep moving forward.

Real or imagined, fear will often prevent us from taking the action necessary to achieve the results we desire.

Developing the Habit of Action

We've already discussed the fact that habits drive an exceptionally high percentage of our daily behaviors. Most of what we do, we do because of habit, especially as it relates to performance and production.

By definition, a habit is a pattern of behavior acquired through frequent repetition. What I'm suggesting is that if we've developed the insidious habit of procrastination, for example, we can, through frequent repetition, develop the counter habit of being action oriented.

Here are some suggestions of how you can develop the habit of taking necessary action at the appropriate time.

1. **Focus on the Present.** Don't reflect on what you did or didn't do yesterday or last week. Both are history and can't be relived. Don't wait for tomorrow. The future is yet to come and probably won't be much different than today in terms of opportunity.

2. **Start Now.** Do what you can with what you have right now. Don't wait for perfect conditions, for just the right equipment, for more money, for assistance, or for permission. You know the line; it's easier to ask for forgiveness than permission, and forgiveness is frequently given.

3. **Intentions Alone Won't Bring Success.** It doesn't matter what you intend to do. What matters is what you actually do. So, make the call, write the proposal, lace up the shoes and hit the road. Don't think about what needs to be done. Take the Nike approach and just do it!

4. Create the Reputation of Being a Doer. I can't think of a more valuable habit to develop than the habit of doing what needs to be done, without being prodded or reminded. Everyone on the planet is looking for and willing to reward those who do what they say they'll do.

In most cases, our performance and productivity will increase dramatically by eliminating those habits that are hindering our success and developing the habits that will guarantee it.

Being an Action-Oriented Person

1. Are you living in the present, or are you spending too much time looking in the rearview mirror, or too far ahead in the future?

2. What negative habits are hindering you from achieving the success and achievement you desire?

3. What positive habits will you develop to counter the ones you identified above?

More Thoughts on Taking Action

"Men acquire a particular quality by constantly acting a particular way … you become just by performing just actions, temperate by performing temperate actions, brave by performing brave actions."

—Aristotle

"An ounce of action is worth a ton of theory."

—Friedrich Engels

"All humanity is divided into three classes: those who are immovable, those who are movable, and those who move!"

—Benjamin Franklin

"The vision must be followed by the venture. It is not enough to stare up the steps—we must step up the stairs."

—Vance Havner

"Never confuse movement with action."

—Ernest Hemingway

"Do not wait; the time will never be 'just right.' Start where you stand, and work with whatever tools you may have at your command, and better tools will be found as you go along."

—Napoleon Hill

"Speech is conveniently located midway between thought and action, where it often substitutes for both."

—John Andrew Holmes

"So what do we do? Anything. Something. So long as we just don't sit there. If we screw it up, start over. Try something else. If we wait until we've satisfied all the uncertainties, it may be too late."

—Lee Iacocca

"You will never stub your toe standing still. The faster you go, the more chance there is of stubbing your toe, but the more chance you have of getting somewhere."

—Charles F. Kettering

"Begin somewhere; you cannot build a reputation on what you intend to do."

—Liz Smith

"Even if it doesn't work, there is something healthy and invigorating about direct action."

—Henry Miller

"We should be taught not to wait for inspiration to start a thing. Action always generates inspiration. Inspiration seldom generates action."

—Frank Tibolt

"We are not put in this world to sit still and know; we are put into it to act."

—Woodrow Wilson

"Do not wait to strike till the iron is hot; but make it hot by striking."

—William Butler Yeats

CHAPTER 17

The Power of Pareto

Think like a man of action, act like a man of thought.
~ Henri Bergson

All actions do not carry equal weight. Some actions we take during the course of a day will have a greater impact on the quality of the day than others. The question becomes: how do we decide which actions will produce the best results?

The Pareto Principle

One of the most effective ways I know of for deciding which actions will provide the highest yields is to apply the Pareto Principle.

This amazing concept was developed in the nineteenth century by an Italian economist named Vilafredo Pareto. The story is told that Pareto developed his principle based on an unequal distribution of wealth he observed in his native country.

The economist observed that 20 percent of the people in his village owned 80 percent of the village's wealth. As he began to study this phenomenon, he saw that these same ratios seemed to apply country-wide. Further study revealed universal implications.

In the mid-twentieth century, efficiency expert and quality management pioneer Dr. Joseph Juran, working in the U.S. and in Japan, developed the concept of "the vital few and the trivial many." This concept held that a minority of causes or effort usually lead to a majority of the results. It also came to be known as the 80/20 Rule.

For example:

- 20% of products result in 80% of a company's profitability
- 20% of defects result in 80% of production problems

- 80% of total sales will come from 20% of the sales team

- 20% of a congregation will provide 80% of church giving

80/20 Thinking

Let's take the Pareto Principle and apply it to improving performance and productivity. Twenty percent of our daily activity will result in 80 percent of our production and productivity. Our goal, therefore, is to identify those vital few activities that will turbocharge output.

This will require a little 80/20 thinking. Instead of just rushing into the day or into the week, set aside some time to reflect on what you're currently doing and what kind of results you're either getting or not getting.

Twenty percent of our daily activity will result in 80 percent of our production and productivity.

It's really not that difficult; 80/20 thinking is strategic thinking. It will involve an honest assessment of your life or your job in terms of desired results. I know you already buy into the idea that if you keep doing what you're doing, you'll keep getting what you're getting. That's probably why you're reading this book. Put Pareto to work for you. In terms of your personal health and well-being, what few things could you be doing that would result in a healthier lifestyle?

On the professional side, identify 20 percent of the activities you're currently involved in at work that would significantly improve your performance and productivity at the end of the day or week. Share these concepts with your boss or a coworker and see if they'll work with you on identifying the vital few activities that will reap such bountiful rewards.

80/20 Time Management

Here's a very practical way to use the Pareto Principle as a time management tool. Dedicate 20 percent of your workday to the activities that will produce high-level results.

Under this scenario, if you work an eight-hour day, you'd carve out roughly ninety minutes to work on your highest priorities. Here's even better news: it doesn't have to be ninety continuous minutes. It could be two forty-five minute sessions or three thirty-minute segments. It really doesn't matter. What does matter is that you're uninterrupted and focused on the high payoff activity.

An hour-and-a-half a day, focused on your highest priorities, will produce immediate positive results.

Improving performance personally, professionally, physically, or spiritually is not difficult to do. It's simply a matter of applying 80/20 thinking to every aspect of your life.

Putting Pareto to Work

1. Identify three activities/actions you could take personally that would significantly improve personal performance.

2. Identify three activities/actions you could take personally that would significantly improve professional performance and productivity.

3. Carve out a ninety-minute segment of your day (today) to work on those things that matter most.

Improving performance personally, professionally, physically or spiritually is not difficult to do. It's simply a matter of applying 80/20 thinking to every aspect of your life.

More Thoughts on Focused Activity

"Be wise in the use of time. The question of life is not, 'How much time have we?' The question is, 'What shall we do with it?'"

—Anna Robertson Brown

"You will never find time for anything. If you want time you must make it."

—Charles Buxton

"Much may be done in those little shreds and patches of time which every day produces, and which most men throw away."

—Charles Caleb Colton

"Time is the scarcest resource, and unless it is managed, nothing else can be managed."

—Peter F. Drucker

"Time is really the only capital that any human being has, and the one thing that he cannot afford to lose."

—Thomas Edison

"The number of needless tasks that are performed daily by thousands of people is amazing."

—Henry Ford

"You can only manage time in those moments when you are alert to what is going on within you and around you."

—James T. McCay

"Most time is wasted, not in hours, but in minutes. A bucket with a small hole in the bottom gets just as empty as a bucket that is deliberately kicked over."

—Paul J. Meyer

"How you spend your time is more important than how you spend your money. Money mistakes can be corrected, but time is gone forever."

—David B. Norris

"Without the management of time, you will soon have nothing left to manage."

—William D. Reiff

"Time is the coin of your life. It is the only coin you have, and only you can determine how it will be spent. Be careful lest you let other people spend it for you."

—Carl Sandburg

"There is no such thing in anyone's life as an unimportant day."

—Alexander Woollcott

CHAPTER 18

You Can Conquer Procrastination

Procrastination is the thief of time.
~ Edward Young

What Is Procrastination?

Procrastination is simply a terrible habit that robs us of the most precious commodity we have, our time.

If you're beating yourself up because procrastination has become the rule of your life instead of an exception, keep reading. The fact is everyone procrastinates to one degree or another.

You can usually tell whether or not you need to do something about this nasty little habit based on the consequences you have to endure because of your failure to act in a timely manner.

The fact is there are internal and external consequences to procrastinating. An internal consequence is the sinking feeling we get deep inside when we missed a deadline or missed an opportunity because we failed to act. This damages self-confidence and self-image.

An external consequence to our procrastination is a project not completed on time, an unfinished report, an important phone call missed, a missed meeting, or a gift that didn't get delivered on time.

When procrastination leaves you feeling discouraged and relationships are suffering, it's time to take action.

When procrastination leaves you feeling discouraged and relationships are suffering, it's time to take action.

There Is Hope

Because we probably agree that procrastination is a habit, and we've discovered that habits are developed through

83

consistent behaviors, we come to the obvious conclusion that, with a little effort, we can change our behavior and minimize procrastination.

Why We Procrastinate

There are a number of reasons why people procrastinate. Here's a short list of some of the primary reasons we put off doing what needs to be done:

1. **Fear of Failure**. If we're afraid that whatever we're supposed to do isn't going to turn out well, or perfect, we'll often procrastinate.

2. **Fear of Success**. It's hard to believe but studies show that some of us procrastinate because we fear what the results of our actions might produce. God forbid that we'd be asked to continue or do more because we've been so successful.

3. **Perfectionism**. Procrastination and perfectionism go hand in hand. This stems from setting expectations too high. Somewhere along the line, we've come to believe that we'll be thought less of if we fall short of perfection. The reality, however, is that few people expect perfection. The greater expectation is that the task would be completed on time.

4. **Because We Can Get Away With It.** Successful stints of procrastination tend to reinforce the behavior. We put something off, it's forgotten about or, better yet, someone else steps up and gets it done and voilà, we're off the hook.

Starve the Vice—Feed the Virtue

As with any other negative habit, the best way to minimize procrastination is to replace it with an opposite behavior. For starters, we can begin by admitting that we do procrastinate, and make a commitment to change. Don't just make a commitment to yourself; ask a friend, coworker, or spouse to hold you accountable.

As with any other negative habit, the best way to minimize procrastination is to replace it with an opposite behavior.

Identify those things that trigger procrastination and find ways to avoid them. The Internet, specifically email, can be the bane of a procrastinator's existence. It's all too easy to lose ourselves in our inbox or to while hours away surfing the Web.

Make a habit of breaking down any project into manageable bits. What's the adage? Inch by inch, anything's a cinch.

Learn to be realistic in estimating the time a particular project will take. Here's a good rule of thumb: the project will probably take longer than you first imagine. Planning is a key element to counter procrastination. A realistic timetable will go a long way in countering procrastination.

Identify those things that trigger procrastination and find ways to avoid them.

Remember the Pareto Principle for time management we talked about earlier, and keep your calendar up-to-date and plug in specific time for working on your project. If possible, keep the calendar in front of you at all times. In Microsoft Outlook, for example, checking your calendar and tasks on a regular basis is a great way to stay focused on what's really important.

See procrastination for what it is, a very bad habit. It will rob you of time you'll never be able to get back. Experiment with various strategies for getting things done in different ways. Ask for help. Find a role model, someone who has developed the habit of getting things done early or on time, and spend time with that person. Learn his or her techniques.

Don't punish yourself when you do procrastinate, but do reward yourself when you don't. Positive reinforcement will go a long way in establishing the feeding of the new habit and starving the old one.

Overpower Procrastination

1. Identify three reasons why you procrastinate.

    1.

    2.

    3.

2. For each reason you identified, develop a strategy for stopping.

3. Identify a task or project you've been procrastinating on and develop a realistic plan for getting it done on time or earlier than expected.

More Thoughts on Procrastination

"No task is a long one but the task on which one dare not start. It becomes a nightmare."

—Charles Baudelaire

"By the streets of 'by and by,' one arrives at the house of 'never.'"

—Miguel de Cervantes

"Know the true value of time; snatch, seize, and enjoy every moment of it. No idleness, no delay, no procrastination; never put off till tomorrow what you can do today."

—Earl of Chesterfield

"Stop procrastinating! I have only to see those words and I'm jerked into starting immediately, because I know only too well from personal experience how easy it is to put off getting down to solid work."

—John Creasy

"If once a man indulges himself in murder, very soon he comes to think little of robbing. And from robbing he comes next to drinking and Sabbath-breaking and from that to incivility and procrastination."

—Thomas De Quincey

"Take action. Procrastination is the death blow to self-motivation. 'I'll do it later …after I get organized' is the language of the unsuccessful and the frustrated. Successful, highly motivated men and women don't put it off. They know their lives are no more than the accumulation of precious seconds, minutes, and days—golden moments never to be recaptured."

—Ted W. Engstrom

"Procrastination is opportunity's natural assassin."

—Victor Kiam

"No unwelcome tasks become any the less unwelcome by putting them off till tomorrow."

—Alexander MacLaren

"Look to today. Procrastination is the art of keeping up with yesterday."

—Don Marquis

"Procrastination is like a credit card: it's a lot of fun until you get the bill."

—Christopher Parker

"Only put off until tomorrow what you are willing to die having left undone."

—Pablo Picasso

"Procrastination is the grave in which opportunity is buried."

—Author Unknown

Section Four: Maintain Alignment

CHAPTER 19

Making Course Adjustments

If you can't measure it, you can't manage it.
~ Anonymous

Alignment is the term we use for making performance or behavioral adjustments as an individual or organization moves from activity to achievement. In the effort to make sure our belief and our behavior are in sync, and in order to achieve the goals we want to achieve, adjustments must be made on a continual basis.

Here's an example from NASA of just how important course adjustments are:

After a rocket launch, mission control at NASA spends most of its time making adjustments to the course of the vehicle.

The moon is 240,000 miles away from the earth. Mission control can land vehicles on the surface of the moon with amazing accuracy. Each mission starts with an extensive written plan for successful completion. Then, from the time the space vehicle is launched until the moment it lands on target, NASA spends 99 percent of its time adjusting the flight plan because of unforeseen circumstances.

Once in space, a rocket encounters equipment malfunctions and various obstacles from asteroids to space junk all along the way. Whether due to an equipment malfunction, or a piece of a planet shooting through space, adjustments must be made to the original plan.

No Success Without Adjustments

Between 1965 and 1969, I served in the United States Navy as a quartermaster or navigator's assistant.

During those four years, I served on the USS Ranger, a thousand-foot-long aircraft carrier, and the USS Dubuque, a much smaller ship capable of navigating in large rivers.

In the case of both vessels, we would spend weeks charting a very detailed course from San Diego, California to the South China Sea, but on each cruise we found ourselves needing to make course adjustments even before we were out of the harbor.

As detailed as our plans might have been, and they were quite detailed, we still had to plan on making course adjustments.

Whether trying to land a spacecraft on the moon or getting a ship from one port to another, course adjustments must be made. There are no exceptions.

> *Whether trying to land a spacecraft on the moon or getting a ship from one port to another, course adjustments must be made. There are no exceptions.*

The Ideal vs. Reality

Remember, strategies, goals, and actions are written descriptions of what we expect to happen. Our strategies describe how we intend to bring our vision to fruition, our goals are designed to measure our progress, and our action plans describe the actual tasks we'll do to accomplish our goals.

As we examine our dreams for the ideal, we must also keep in mind that we don't live in a perfect world. Circumstances change, and in our world things change pretty quickly.

In Spencer Johnson's terrific little book, *Who Moved My Cheese?*, we're reminded of the reality of change in our day-to-day environment.

Dr. Johnson doesn't make change anything other than a common occurrence; something which should be expected and planned for.

The Importance of Alignment

As illustrated in landing a vehicle on the moon or charting a course from San Diego to Vietnam, maintaining alignment by making course adjustments is critical to a successful outcome.

Here a few reasons why maintaining alignment is so important:

- Alignment turns intentions into actions.

- Alignment creates the linkage between the ideal and reality.

- Alignment connects people with performance.

- Alignment creates a culture of success and achievement.

Maintaining alignment means we're able to turn our intentions into actions. We're able to make those continuous adjustments that keep our behavior in sync with our beliefs.

There's nothing wrong with being idealistic as long as we stay in touch with reality. Everything starts as a dream or an idea. Making the dream a reality requires adjusting to life's twists and turns.

As we make the necessary adjustments to our plan and personal performance, we dramatically increase our chances for success.

Alignment is the methodology we use to keep our finger on the pulse of our desired intentions and actions. Measuring progress on an ongoing basis is critical to success and achievement.

> *As we make the necessary adjustments to our plan and personal performance, we dramatically increase our chances for success.*

Measuring and Managing

1. On a scale of 1 to 10, how would you rate your ability to change or adjust?

   1 2 3 4 5 6 7 8 9 10

2. Have you factored in the need to change and/or make course adjustments to your current plan for improving performance and productivity?

3. Read *Who Moved My Cheese?* and apply the concepts to your current program for personal or professional achievement.

More Thoughts on Maintaining Course

"Change is a process and not a destination, it never ends!"
—James Belasco

"We cannot direct the wind, but we can adjust the sails."
—Bertha Calloway

"Since changes are going on anyway, the great thing is to learn enough about them so that we will be able to lay hold of them and turn them in the direction of our desires."
—John Dewey

"Without goals, and plans to reach them, you are like a ship that has set sail with no destination."

—Fitzhugh Dodson

"The pessimist complains about the wind. The optimist expects it to change. The leader adjusts the sails."

—John C. Maxwell

"One ship drives East, and one drives West, by the selfsame wind that blows. It's the set of the sails, and not the gales, which determines the way it goes."

—Ella Wheeler Wilcox

CHAPTER 20

✦

The Elements of Alignment

The important thing is to start,
to lay a plan and then follow it step-by-step no matter
how small or large each step by itself may seem.
—Robert Louis Stevenson

There are two primary elements of alignment:

1. Horizontal Alignment
2. Vertical Alignment

Horizontal alignment ensures our belief (perspective) and our behavior (performance) are in sync. Horizontal alignment means our mission is in alignment with our vision. It means our values complement our vision and define our behavior.

Our strategies, goals, and actions (behavior) are in direct alignment with our belief system. Our *strategies* complement our vision, our *objectives* quantify our strategic initiatives, and our *action plans* ensure that we'll take the necessary actions and establish the specific tasks to accomplish our goals.

Vertical alignment links our strategy and our staff. Jim Collins, in his classic book, *Good To Great*, maintained that organizations move from good to great by having the right people in the right seats to make sure the organization accomplishes what needs to be accomplished.

Collins also says people are not our most important asset, but rather the right people, in the right seats, are an organization's most important asset.

Maintaining Alignment Is a Team Sport

Alignment isn't just the responsibility of a single individual in an organization. There'll be a number of fingerprints all over alignment. Here are a few of the realities of alignment:

- Alignment is an ongoing process.

- Alignment should be applied to every step of the process from casting our vision of what we want to accomplish to taking the necessary actions to bring the vision to fruition.

- Alignment requires the right "gauges."

- Alignment is the role of leadership and management.

As I mentioned earlier, course adjustments must be made from the very beginning to the absolute end of the performance improvement process. Alignment is a never-ending process.

Course adjustments must be made from the very beginning to the absolute end of the performance improvement process. Alignment is a never-ending process.

While our perspective (beliefs) will require minimal adjustments, our performance (behavior) will require constant review and regular tweaks. Adjustments to a well-designed plan will be, for the most part, minor in nature.

Gauges refer to the methodologies we use to maintain alignment. Gauges typically take the form of reports and meetings—reports that are able to identify key metrics, and meetings which include the right people. In addition to the right people, meetings must have the appropriate format; one designed to elicit the right information.

Alignment Is the Role of Both Leaders and Managers

If developing perspective is the role of leadership and defining performance is the role of management and staff, then maintaining alignment is the role of leadership and management, both working together to make sure that belief and behavior are in sync.

The distinction between the role of leadership and management is nowhere better demonstrated than in following illustration provided by Dr. Warren Bennis in his fabulous book, *On Becoming a Leader*.

In the book, Dr. Bennis clarifies these primary distinctions between the role of the leader and the manager.

Maintaining alignment is the role of leadership and management, both working together to make sure that belief and behavior are in sync.

A Leader	A Manager
Innovates	Administers
Develops	Maintains
Focuses on People	Focuses on Systems and Structures
Inspires Trust	Relies on Control
Asks "What and Why?"	Asks "How and When?"
Originates	Initiates
Does the "Right" Things	Does Things "Right"

These distinctions have nothing to do with the worth of an individual in either role. Both leadership and management are critical to an organization's success. It simply points out that the leader and the manager do different things.

In many cases, these two roles overlap. Leaders must be able to manage, and managers must demonstrate some degree of leadership. In order to maintain alignment, leaders and managers must work together while also fulfilling their unique roles and responsibilities.

The Overlap

- Innovation requires administration.

- Development requires maintenance.

- People need systems and structure to be effective.

- The trust a leader develops secures control.

- Both leaders and managers need to ask the right questions.

- Lastly, both need to do the right thing, the right way.

While the principle of alignment might seem somewhat philosophical, applying this principle is absolutely critical to success and achievement.

What we say we believe must be seen in our behavior. In fact, one of the major disconnects in individuals and organizations is not living the professed belief system. Like it or not, people are watching. Behavior is the litmus test for belief.

Now It's Your Turn

Look at your life or the life of your business and ask the hard question: Are my beliefs and behaviors in alignment?

1. Are your vision, mission, and values in alignment? Are they congruent and complementary?

2. Are your strategies, goals, and actions stated in such a way they create a clear picture of what's to be achieved, establish measurable objectives, and define necessary action items?

3. Do your leadership and management roles overlap? Or, are you leaning too heavily on one side or the other?

More Thoughts on Alignment

"Leadership is the initiation and direction of endeavor in the pursuit of consequence."
—Royal Alcott

"Cooperation is the thorough conviction that nobody can get there unless everybody gets there."
—Virginia Burden

"The conscientious plodder is nearly always outdistanced by the fellow who stops occasionally to analyze and plan."
—W.J. Cameron

"Teamwork is the ability to work together toward a common vision. The ability to direct individual accomplishments toward organizational objectives. It is the fuel that allows common people to attain uncommon results."
—Andrew Carnegie

"Good things happen only when planned. Bad things happen on their own."
—Philip B. Crosby

"All winning teams are goal-oriented. Teams like these win consistently because everyone connected with them concentrates on specific objectives. They go about their business with blinders on; nothing will distract them from achieving their aims."

—Lou Holtz

"Leadership is important because it's all about direction. True leaders help us move forward."

—Dan Kahl

"Plan your progress carefully; hour-by hour, day-by-day, month-by-month. Organized activity and maintained enthusiasm are the wellsprings of your power."

—Paul J. Meyer

"In strategy it is important to see distant things as if they were close and to take a distanced view of close things."

—Miyamoto Musashi

CHAPTER 21

❈

What You Believe, You Can Achieve

Think of yourself as on the threshold of unparalleled success.
A whole clear, glorious life lies before you. Achieve! Achieve!
—*Andrew Carnegie*

Mary Kathlyn Wagner was born in a small Texas town in 1918. Married at age twenty-five, she and her husband had three children. After a divorce, she went to work in direct sales but quit when a man she had trained was promoted over her, at twice the salary. So, with $5,000 and the help of her twenty-year-old son, Richard Rogers, she launched her own business.

The rest, as they say, is history. At the time of her death in 2001, the company she founded, Mary Kay Cosmetics, had 800,000 representatives in thirty-seven countries, with annual sales in excess of two billion dollars.

What was it that propelled Mary Kay Ash, honored as one of the greatest female entrepreneurs in American history, to such heights? "Don't limit yourself," she said. "Many people limit themselves to what they think they can do. You can go as far as your mind lets you. What you believe, remember, you can achieve."

I began this book by sharing with you my commitment to simplicity and to fundamentals. I've come to learn from personal and professional experience that success and achievement do *not* require complicated formulas and methodologies. What you believe, you can indeed achieve!

Moving from Activity to Achievement is a simple but very powerful construction for seeing success and achievement in virtually any endeavor. The six steps and three principles described in the previous chapters of this book establish the fundamentals for linking belief and behavior.

Perspective helps us clarify *what* we want to accomplish by simplifying our vision. Once we've clearly defined what we want to accomplish or where we want to go, we've taken a giant step in moving toward what we know will satisfy and fulfill.

Being able to articulate *why* we're moving in a particular direction is both motivating and inspiring. It's motivating to us and it's inspiring to those who will help us achieve our stated vision.

Identifying those few *core values* that will define our behavior, individually and organizationally, creates a constitution of sorts, which declares to friends, family, colleagues, and clients how we intend to be and how we intend to serve.

Defining Performance

Defining performance moves us from the believing stage to the doing stage. It forces us to take three simple steps toward making our dreams and aspirations realities.

Strategies add further clarity to how we will bring our vision to fruition. There are several moving parts to getting us from where we are now to where we want to be. If it's a healthier lifestyle we'll need nutritional strategies, exercise strategies, and we'll need to expand our scope of knowledge of how our bodies respond to various foods and various types of fitness.

If we want to move our organization from activity to achievement, we'll need to have sales strategies, marketing strategies, and process improvement strategies. We'll have to clearly define how we'll recruit, train, and effectively utilize the men and women who make up our organization.

Goals become the fuel we need to move us to action by quantifying what we'll need to accomplish to make our vision and our strategies a reality. By being very specific about what we want to accomplish and establish realistic deadlines, we energize our dreams. A hope is not a goal!

Actions prove our intentions. Our behavior demonstrates how committed we are to our stated beliefs. Ashley Montagu was exactly right when he said, "If you want to know what people believe … just observe what they do."

It's All About You!

So in the end, it all boils down to personal action and personal commitment. The person most responsible for your success and well-being is *you*. It's not the government, it's not your parents, and it's not your boss or your colleagues. It's only up to you! Others may take credit for what you do, they may even take the blame for what you didn't do, but when all the feathers hit the floor, it's simply your choice to move from activity to achievement.

You now have the process you need to take yourself or your company to new levels of success and achievement. You now have six simple steps and three powerful principles for improving performance, productivity, and profitability.

Thank you for reading this book. I encourage you to apply what you've learned to your personal or professional life, or both. The simple truths I've shared have helped hundreds if not thousands of others achieve phenomenal levels of success and achievement.

Just remember, achievement is about doing, not about dreaming. Develop perspective, define performance, and maintain alignment.

ABOUT THE AUTHOR

Les Taylor is a professional speaker, author, consultant, and recognized expert in the field of personal improvement and professional development. With over three decades of success and achievement in both the public and private sectors, Les Taylor is uniquely qualified to help individuals and organizations improve performance and productivity, both personally and professionally.

Les served as the assistant chief of police in Tempe, Arizona, and retired in 1993 to become the executive director of the Arizona Association of Chiefs of Police. After leaving law enforcement, Les traveled internationally, presenting seminars on ethical leadership on four continents.

As the president and CEO of Achievement Solutions, Les is now helping individuals and organizations improve performance, productivity, and profitability by introducing them to time-tested principles for success and achievement.

Les may be contacted by email at les@lestaylor.net, or visit his Web site at www.achievement-solutions.com.